17
Hours
Tracking Down Our Runaway

DIANE M. BASSETT

DENVER, COLORADO

Outskirts Press, Inc.
http://www.outskirtspress.com

ISBN: 978-1-4787-7489-1

Library of Congress Control Number: 2016905695

Outskirts Press and the "OP" logo are trademarks belonging to Outskirts Press, Inc.

PRINTED IN THE UNITED STATES OF AMERICA

This Book is dedicated to God…

You call me to write; may the eyes you want to read this,
find it in time to help

Acknowledgments

Samantha: This is your story, and your blessing to tell it so that it might help other families is a testament to your growth. I love you. I will always be your biggest fan in life, believing there isn't anything you can't do. From the day I met you in your mommy's belly, I was connected to you. Raising you, and finally adopting you, were simply what I was called to do. Thank you for making it such an interesting journey!

GoFundMe Supporters: I believe they used to call you benefactors. D.W., Wolter Portier, Gary Geister, Mom and Dad, Vicki VanSteenwyk, Jennifer Bejcek, J. B., Elayne Dimmitt, Janelle Fletcher…you all put your money on the line and believed in what I was doing. You made it possible to get this book printed immediately. Thank you for giving my calling the means to be heard.

Friends and Family: There is no substitute for the boost your words of encouragement gave me. When reliving this experience got me down, I could go on Facebook or read your emails and my spirits brightened. I have an amazing network of very treasured people around me; I hope you include yourself amongst them!

Diane

Table Of Contents

*I have tried to recreate events, locales and conversations from my memories of them. In order to maintain their anonymity in some instances I have changed the names of individuals and places, I may have changed some identifying characteristics and details such as physical properties, occupations and places of residence.

Foreword

The reasons a child runs away are as varied as the number of children that run each year, estimated to be a staggering 1.6 million youths by one report (1800runaway.org), even higher according to Youth.gov, who estimate between 500,000 and 2.5 million youths are on the streets any given year (youth.gov). Being a teenager is rarely easy, and for some, the multitude of issues culminate in a single point in time being the breaking point where life on the streets is preferable to life in the home. The challenge as parents is to get them where they'll be safe. All other issues can be dealt with once they're off the streets. If they need drug or alcohol rehabilitation, mental health counseling, finding another option for living--those are all issues that can be dealt with once the child is no longer being exposed to the risks the streets pose to our youths, particularly our female youths.

For our daughter Samantha, her reasons for running away had been building since birth, and yet exploded into running away only when what she heard me say during an argument wasn't what I said at all. That miscommunication, which was typical but not dealt with in our home, was the root cause of her running. Communication was so poor among us three that in looking back I'm surprised she didn't jump sooner. Had our communication been better, she could have felt safe telling us about her attack in our home, the continued harassment she was suffering, the new men in her life and what they were asking/telling her to do. But because we three rarely openly communicated, the pressure and lies became too much for her, and she jumped out of the window to get away from it all when what she heard me say would have meant everything being exposed. I accept my blame in her running away. I didn't listen well enough; I wasn't hearing her. I wasn't checking up on her. I was trusting her in spite of concerns.

Born to my second husband's oldest daughter Jessica, Samantha had lived with us off and on her first year of life, and eventually came to live with us permanently when she was just shy of her second birthday. In spite of our providing her a stable and loving home, she still coped with more than her share of childhood trauma. A small sampling of her childhood includes a physical disability, a change of fathers after a court-ordered DNA test, a name change, multiple abandonments, and two cases of juvenile PTSD; she returned from visits with bruises and a black eye, and had been bullied throughout her school years for being different.

There hadn't been a single school year since kindergarten that hadn't involved school counselors, principals, suspensions, special sitting areas for her anger fits, school guards, or police. No technique or plan had ever lasted one full school year.

When Sam was in third grade I was in my car waiting for her after school when I saw the principal come out of the building. She was holding a white envelope in her hand and started walking toward the line of cars parked across the street where I waited for Sam every day. I knew without a doubt the white envelope was meant for me, so I wasn't surprised when she approached my car. I already had the window down. She handed me the envelope and explained why she felt Sam needed to stay home for two days. I nodded where appropriate, because there wasn't much to say. Sam had broken into a locked closet and stolen the teacher's answer guide, one of only three for this Junior Achievement project for the entire third grade, and had taken it home. I had received a call from an exasperated principal who was pretty sure Sam had it at home. I checked her room, and it was there.

I returned it and they had told me they would think about what her punishment would be. So a principal walking toward you with a white envelope... roll that window down Momma, it's for you. She was still a little kid and yet I had already gone through more with her than my other two children combined. At night, though, when the letters and emails about my child were answered, when the angry neighborhood moms demanding she never darken their doorstep with her presence again had gone home to their perfect worlds, that child would curl into me and look up at me with those green eyes and I was helpless against my need to protect her. From the world, and from herself.

She seemed to come through it all tougher than ever as she aged, but that turned out to be wishful thinking on my part. In spite of regular counseling throughout her childhood with a superb counselor and family friend to help her cope with her experiences, Samantha still jumped out the window. Even though I am a child advocate, educated and trained in helping children, she still jumped out the window. Even though she enjoys a close relationship with my husband, she still jumped out the window. No one is immune. No family is immune. The National Conference of State Legislatures estimates that 1 in 7 people between the ages of 10 and 18 will run away, and that 75% of those youth are female (ncsl.org). Given those statistics and Sam's childhood experiences, I probably should have expected she'd run at some point during her childhood. I didn't; I thought I was more in tune with her than I really was. I thought my education and training would make it impossible for any real issues to go unnoticed, and yet they did. The reality is that what goes on inside a teenager's brain that makes them run away is as different as the teens themselves. They will show you only those parts of themselves they want you to see; you have to be watching carefully to get the whole picture.

What Samantha was hiding from us was a trauma she kept to herself: a rape while I was out of town. We wouldn't learn about that until after months of post-running counseling. But it was that untreated trauma, paired with her childhood, combined with her exposure to sex traffickers at her local park, and an inability to communicate it all to us that led Samantha out that window.

I asked Samantha when I began this project what her reasons were for running. It's been almost a year and I thought with her new perspective she might finally be able to explain some things that didn't make sense, like the runaway letter. Sam's response now to why she ran away is different than it was a year ago when she made that choice. I expect it will change again as she ages. She tells me now that she isn't sure why she did, she just felt the need that particular night to go. I asked her how much of what we were told about her double life activities during those seventeen hours was factual. She says not much, but the forwarded texts and messages that came in from her school friends during our search, as well as counselor reports from juvenile detention, rehab, and after care counseling indicate more accuracy than maybe she's able to cope with right now. The reports all point toward many years of therapy ahead to unravel what really happened. We may never know; it may not be for us to know. That's Sam's story to tell. She has to live with it; all we can do is love and support her while she copes with what happened to her.

This book isn't about Samantha's unique life or experiences, though; it's about what was done in an incredibly short period of time to get her back, what we could have improved on, and some things you might not have thought of and can use if you ever find yourself in the position of having to track down a runaway. The longer a child remains on the streets, the less chance the parents have of getting them back at all. With today's technology, the ability to track down a child is easier than ever before. The hope is this will be read before it's needed, and that some of the information will be used, and found useful in the recovery of another child from the streets. There's a Quick Tip Guide (QTG) in the back to answer the first question after a child runs away that I asked myself: "What do I do?" The QTG will give you some direction as you begin your own journey to locating a runaway. If you are helping to locate a runaway child, please pass the QTG along to those searching.

If you're a parent who will do anything for your child's well-being, you'll identify with our seventeen hours.

The Hours Before

I was waiting for Sam to return from her friend's house, if that's even where she had been. I never really knew for sure these days. Sam had been distant and sneaky for months. Getting her up for homeschool had been next to impossible. She always had a good reason: period cramps all night, the trains were louder than usual, stress over a girlfriend's poor choice of boyfriend, or my personal favorite—"I'm just a teenager, I sleep a lot." She'd even gone so far as to use my daughter Kate as a teenager as her example of why she needed so much extra sleep. Kate was famous in the family for napping so long she required a nap from her nap. Recently Sam had been claiming she was just like Kate, and simply needed lots of sleep. It was plausible enough to believe.

Lately, though, she had been doing her schoolwork wrapped in a blanket, rarely getting out of her pajamas. It had been a sore point for us and one I was tired of fighting about. I wanted to see her dressed and motivated like I was when I finished school on my own from my kitchen table. I had taken pride in doing a great job to prove to my parents my decision to complete high school through correspondence was a good choice. I wanted Sam to care about her schooling like I did. I wasn't expecting her to be an honor student, but to at least show she cared. She had gotten into serious trouble at the local high school so I was home schooling her for the duration of her tenth-grade year. She had to make it through only two more months and we could call it good for the school year. We'd be straggling to the finish line, but we'd make it there if I had to drag her along for the journey.

I talked to Sam weekly about keeping her nose clean and staying out of trouble so she could get through the probation period from her latest slip of judgment. This round had been the worst to date and I wasn't sure I could handle much more trouble from her. She reassured me daily that she was taking pride in being good. I could relax; she wasn't going to put me through any more. She promised. She would cup my face in her hands, stare into my eyes, tell me she was being good, kiss me on the tip of my nose, and I ate it up like a starving parent. I believed every word. I was worn out from dealing with her constant issues and I had chosen to retreat to a world of computers and network marketing. It was easier just to assume she was behaving, and far easier than dealing with Gary over her. He was knee-deep in a large downtown building project and was rarely mentally present even when he was home. Our dining room table was regularly piled up with his paperwork and notebooks during the weekends as he worked to get on top of the next big project. We were three separate lives operating under one roof. We were aware of her attitude change, but her constant denials of anything being wrong won out over either of us taking the time to dig deeper. Sometimes lies are just easier to believe than the truth is to dig out. No matter what we asked, she handed us a pile of lies, we smiled and nodded, she left, I headed for my computer, and her dad dove into his paperwork. If you had asked us at any given point where our daughter was, we would have been hard-pressed to tell you. We could tell you where she said she'd be, but we never followed up and went and physically checked that she was where she claimed to be.

Until May 25, 2015 when the option of digging deeper became a matter of her life or death.

5/25/2015 9:00 p.m.

Sam walked in the door and I told her to sit down at the dining room table. We had been through this so many times before--years of sitting at the table talking about what was wrong and why she needed to stop making poor choices. We each took in a long deep breath and got ready to start our accusation/denial dance. I glanced at my watch to make sure I had time to deal with the matter before Gary got home. He doesn't do well with confrontations and conflict, so some things were best handled before he returned, especially after working all day and attending a foreman's meeting all evening. It was a bad habit I had gotten into less than a year after Sam came to live with us. It made life easier if he wasn't a part of any discussions where there would be conflict or where denials would be introduced. And knowing Sam and what I was about to talk to her about, denials were forthcoming. I wanted to deal with it, end it on a good note with her re-motivated, and get her busy with her homework before her dad came in the door.

I asked her about taking more out of the ATM with my bank card than she had been approved to. I regularly trusted Samantha with my bank card, and she had always been really good about turning in the receipt with the card. This time, however, she didn't have a receipt and claimed the ATM hadn't given her one. It hadn't made sense to me, so while she was gone I pulled up my bank account information and saw that the $100 withdrawal had been made for $120. Her response to my question was to make a snarky response about me not trusting her. I told her I no longer believed that the ATM failed to give a receipt as she had claimed, but that she had thrown it away so that I wouldn't see the total withdrawn. She squeezed some tears to the corners of her eyes and began fervently denying any wrongdoing. I reminded her that she was on probation for some pretty serious charges and that I was in no mood to listen to lies nor to dig for the truth. She said she understood, that she swore she hadn't taken out more than the $100 I had asked for, and she was really hurt that I was once again not believing her. The tears now spilled over onto her cheeks and she wiped them away as if she was being brave in the face of accusations.

I asked her if she was done yet. She said she just needed me to know she wasn't lying, that she hadn't stolen from me, that she'd been making good choices as promised, and that this was just one accusation too many. She simply couldn't take living where she wasn't trusted. She laid her head down on her folded arms and sobbed some incoherent words about how my lack of trust in her tore her apart. I watched the performance for a minute and was impressed with the quality of her work. She was really throwing herself into the role of accused teenager and giving me a full show for my money. I told her we'd go to the bank in the morning to settle it by checking their camera footage. She suddenly grew very quiet and raised her head to look at me.

"What?" she asked. She wiped her nose and studied me with a steady gaze. It was amazing how quickly those tears dried up.

"We can settle this quite easily, Sam, no argument. We'll go to the bank and view their footage of your ATM visit. It will show us how much you took out and that a receipt never printed, as you claim."

Sam got very still and quietly said, "Oh."

"Care to change your story yet? Given that there's footage, given that there's a record, and given that I've already viewed the withdrawal on my iPad and KNOW you took out $120?" I presented my proof like a lawyer in the courtroom.

Sam burst into a fresh set of tears and started screaming at me that this was all bullshit. She hadn't taken the money and my disbelief was crap.

Just then Gary walked in and stood with his hands on his hips, surveying the scene. Sam was crying, I was sitting across from her staring at her coldly, and my opportunity to handle it without his input disappeared in the blink of an eye. Gary told me that whatever it was we were fighting about to just let it go, which turned the argument between her and me into a new war of words as he and I fought. He refused to believe she had stolen from me. The argument continued for almost half an hour until Sam interrupted us and admitted what I already knew.

"Yes, I took it. Yes, I threw the receipt away. What's the big deal? It was just 20 bucks!"

I stared at Sam. "What's the big deal?" I finally exploded! "The big deal is you're on probation. The big deal is that you stole from me. The big deal is you lied all evening. The big deal is your dad and I are sitting here arguing because you wouldn't admit the truth!" The volume of my voice was rising with each "big deal" reason I came up with.

Sam shrugged her shoulders and stated, "I don't see what the big deal is really."

I thought the veins in my head might explode on the spot. *How can she not get this?! How can she sit there so snotty when she stole from me?!*

I clamped my mouth shut for fear of screaming horrid words at them both, and stepped outside for a cigarette. *How dare she?! I can't believe she's putting us through even more. How much will be enough for her?* I took a long drag and watched the smoke curl up from the end. *God, I hate these things. Nasty habit.* I paced back and forth across the deck. I took another deep drag and looked out at the marina. *Happy people having happy lives. What's that like to have a happy life where finding parking at the marina for your boat is your biggest problem today?* I finished my smoke, tossed it in the metal dragon butt-tender with as much anger toward the marina visitors as toward Sam, and headed back inside.

Gary stood by the table having a talk with Sam. He thanked her for telling the truth. *Telling the truth?!* She smiled at him and left the smile on her face as she turned back toward me. Anger flooded me and I couldn't even stand to look at her. I turned to head to my room, but left her with some parting words to think about. These parting words became directly responsible for Sam choosing this night to run away. I told Sam I would be calling her probation officer in the morning to discuss it, and that we'd leave the consequences up to him. If he was fine letting it go, so would I. If he wanted to lock her up for the $20, I'd be okay with that as well. I didn't want to hear her excuses anymore, nor Gary's defense of her, so I excused myself to go work on my iPad in my room.

Sam's Notes-What I heard was "I'm going to call your probation officer and you're going to be locked away for twenty [years]. No way I was going to be locked away for 20 years!"

That miscommunication right there set into motion her need to run. Sam thought she was facing twenty years for theft, that the men she was involved with would come looking for her, and that her secrets would all come out. I should have made sure she knew I was talking about twenty bucks and not twenty years.

I could hear her having a chat with her dad in the dining room and everything seemed to be settling down. I'd call her probation officer in the morning; he'd probably let it go, but hopefully the scare would be enough to keep her from doing it again. I could hope, at least. I was just too tired to care either way at the moment.

11:00 p.m.

I opened up my Game of War video game and started to play. I led the OWP clan and had duties to perform each night as their leader. Here on the game I was respected as a fair but fierce competitor and leader--people referred to me as "Queen" and the power was intoxicating. I had total and complete control in my game, and it had become a drug to me. I settled in for my nightly fix, for relaxing hour, my favorite time of the day. The house is typically quiet, all work for the home is completed, and it officially becomes "my" time to play and rest my brain before some much-needed sleep.

Sam passed by my bedroom on her way upstairs. I heard her stop outside of my door. "Good night, Mom. I love you."

"I love you too," I responded, but quietly and without any emotion. *She can go to bed knowing how disappointed in her I am.* I heard her footsteps heading upstairs and went back to being "Queen Book." I was enjoying chatting and monster-bashing with Drako, Jammin, Ghost, Foot, and Doc--and at the moment that seemed endlessly more fun than dealing with a sulky teenager yet again.

Sam's Notes-I didn't hear Mom say anything that night when I went upstairs. I went to bed thinking I had said I love you and she didn't say anything in return.

11:15 p.m.

I became aware Gary hadn't gone to bed yet. We had separate beds in one large room and he was usually in bed by 9:00 p.m. The fight had kept us all up late, but past 10:00 p.m. was unheard-of for him. I grabbed my water bottle and headed to the kitchen to refill it and check on him. I found him sitting in the dark on the stairs. "What are you doing?" I asked. He waved me away with a shushing sound, so I headed to the kitchen and then back to my room without talking to him again. It was strange to see him on the stairs, but not unheard-of for him to listen in on conversations from outside a room. I figured he was just listening to Sam talking on her computer upstairs, and ignored him. I was still angry at his reaction to her theft and I didn't really care what he was doing or why. I headed back to my game and my clansmen. I needed some ego-stroking and I knew right where to go to get it.

A commotion on the stairs grabbed my attention. I closed my iPad just as Gary threw open the bedroom door. "She's gone!" he shouted as he raced past my bed to the closet. For a split second the air in the room seemed as thick as oatmeal and his words buzzed in my ears. *Did he just say she's gone?!*

HOUR 1:

It Begins With A Jump…

11:30 p.m.-12:30 a.m.

"What do you mean she's gone?" I ask him as I jump up and grab my pants. I'm putting them on as Gary paces back and forth across the room.

"Sam. She just jumped out her window, she's gone!" Gary throws on his sweatshirt and grabs his keys off his dresser. *I've never seen him look so scared.* "I have to go find her--I knew this would happen!" He's out the door before I have a chance to ask any questions, or point out that he has no shoes on.

I walk out to the dining room and stand there at a loss for what to do. I see the Jeep racing up the street in the dark. What do I do? My mind is blank. What do I do? Do I call someone? Who? Old television movies about runaways start racing through my thoughts. What was their advice? What did they do? *I don't need to worry about that; she'll be back. This is just yet another Sam stunt. Her poor dad will drive the streets for a while until she's had her fun, and then she'll come home, and be real sorry and he'll forgive her.* I let out a heavy sigh. Would this child ever get that her trouble took more effort than just following the rules would take?

I find myself in the kitchen and make a fresh pot of coffee to keep busy. While it brews, I pace back and forth to the living room window to see if Gary's back with Sam. *He'll be back any minute with her. We'll scold her for this and we'll all go to bed. It'll all be fine by morning.* I wipe down the counters and straighten things up, looking for anything to take my mind off what's happening. Sam's done a lot of things over the years, but jumping from her window and running off in the night is all new. *This just couldn't be because of the ATM talk. It couldn't be. It wasn't that serious. This doesn't make any sense!*

I walk by the dining room table and see her homework sitting there with two school books. I don't remember seeing them when we were at the table earlier. Were they left because she wouldn't be back? For the first time tonight I experience a gut cramp that warns me this may be different. *Sam never has her homework done early, and why are her books out here? She hasn't even started them yet this semester, so why are they out here?* I stand and stare down at her homework on the table. The little pile seems so strange and out of place; I can't even focus on what it says because I'm so struck by its appearance there.

When Sam was in sixth grade her behavior had become so intrusive on other students and their ability to learn that I chose to keep her home for seventh grade. When I told her, she responded with wide eyes, "But you can't do that! School is where my friends are; it's where my life is." I had responded, "Then you should have taken more care with the privilege. I may not be able to sing like Madonna, but I can certainly keep your butt home for a year and homeschool you." And I had, for her entire seventh grade. We fought like cats and dogs the entire school year, but she successfully completed the year and was released by me to go back to public school. When she returned to her local school in eighth grade she was an honor-roll student with excellent study habits. She and I struck a deal: No more school trouble, or I'd homeschool her again clear through graduation the next time. I had already proven I would homeschool her if needed, so the threat held a great deal of weight. A simple reminder always seemed to snap her back into line and her tardies or skipped classes would diminish for a week or two. Unfortunately, the effects never seemed to last permanently, and the struggle with Sam and school would resume after a short break.

She had pushed my limits since returning for eighth grade, but after being called to the school twice this year by Officer Harris, I had pulled her for the duration of her tenth-grade school year and had been homeschooling her once again. The hope was to give her time to settle down like she had done in seventh grade, while giving me a break from apologizing to school staff for her behavior. The truth was, though, that this time it was a daily struggle to get her to stay awake and do her classes. She was blowing off important classes and projects, showing up at the table still in pajamas at 10:00 in the morning; the result was this time it wasn't working out very well. Every attempt I made at correction, suggestion, or demands that she be dressed and ready were met with cold stares and yawns. If I pushed too hard she would slam her fists on the table, rise up, and stand over me, screaming uncontrollably. My only recourse had been to go drill sergeant on her, rise up, and scream her back into her seat so we could continue. I couldn't let her threaten me like that, but maintaining peace and order was becoming more physical and frightening with her. There were times I was truly afraid I was about to get her fist in my face, but so far she had always backed down, calmed down, we had talked it out, and continued on.

With her legal troubles, though, homeschool was Sam's last schooling option available for the year. If she returned to the local high school, she would owe them thirty days' suspension; however, they didn't really want her back and made that clear. She hated homeschool, but hadn't taken the necessary steps to remain in the local school--like behaving--so she simply had to deal with it. We were barely making it through this school year, but the hope was always the same: keep her on track and pray that age would mature her out of this. So far it hadn't.

11:44 p.m.

Facebook message received from Paul, the father of Sam's friend Mary. "Urgent. I have information on Sam. Please contact me." Because my notifications are regularly turned off with the volume silenced, I did not receive this message until 4:48 a.m.

Lesson Learned: Turn all notifications on and turn up the sound. Do this on every device. You can't be sure when the right person to help you will cross your path.

I check back in with my game for a minute and let the guys know Sam's pulled another stupid stunt. We've been gaming together for over a year and have become such close friends that we call each other "family." They all offer to post notices in their local areas if I need it. Some of them live overseas and I find their immediate willingness to step up and help heartwarming. I thank them and promise to keep them informed, but that I don't expect it to impact my gaming time at all. *She'll be back in an hour or so I'm sure.* I line up a few "generals" to cover for me in case this takes more than the night. I do a few leader duties and log off, anxious for Gary and Sam to get home.

I grab a cup of hot black coffee and sit in the quiet front living room, looking out at the black night. *I caused this. Over $20! But you had to say something; she can't be a thief in life. Maybe not, but now she's out there.* I battle back and forth with myself in my head about the decision to confront her, but eventually logic wins out. *I had to--bottom line. Theft is theft.* I know Gary won't see it that way, and I dread the lecture that's bound to follow her running away. It will be my fault for fighting with her. His first wife battled with Jessica until she ran away, the result being Samantha. *I don't want to see Sam head down that path. Thank goodness I had birth control implanted in her arm!* It brings me some small comfort that at least no child will result from tonight's decisions.

I become aware of the kitchen clock and its ticking noise. I try to block it out, but it begins to bang into my skull, each tick a reminder another tick has passed and they are still out there, somewhere. I can't stand the sound anymore and I snatch it off the wall. I rip the battery out of the back of it so it stops and hang the now-still clock back on the wall and stare at it. It looks like a death clock from the old days. Someone dies, so stop the clock to mark the time. The scene with the death clock from my favorite movie *Fried Green Tomatoes* runs through my head and I wish it hadn't. *Did I just mark Sam's time?*

I pace the house in a big circle--dining room to hall through my bedroom, out the other door into the living room, through the kitchen and back into the dining room. It makes a nice big circle to pace and lose myself in my thoughts. *I'm so pissed. How dare she?! Hurry up and haul her butt home so I can get back to my game, Gary. She's caused enough drama with her choices for one day. But then again my baby's out there in the night. Where are you, boo?!* I swing between anger and fear by the minute.

In this town at night there is almost no activity or traffic, so every car sounds like a fire engine going by. The noise stands out and echoes off the buildings in the two-block downtown area. With only a few thousand residents, every car passing the house causes my heart to stop. There aren't many cars. Each time I race to the window and look out, hoping it's Gary and Sam. The three that pass by aren't who I'm hoping to see. I step outside and light another cigarette. I don't think one ever tasted quite so good. *Man what a night! Yes, we can officially classify this night as SUCK.* How many times had I stood out here, smoking away the latest drama? *I'm so tired of the problems. I can't do this; I'm not a healthy person.* Family members had raised concerns in the past that raising Samantha might be too hard on my body. *They may have a point. The smoking doesn't help.*

Exposed to a full-body X-ray when I was five months old in the womb, my medical life had been different from day one. It seemed I was constantly in a state of battling the latest diagnosis. My family had expressed concerns for years that Samantha's behavior was too taxing on me physically and I might need to explore other options for her upbringing. However, it quickly became apparent when Sammy was young that there was no one else willing to raise her; we were the best option this kid had, and we were determined to make it work. Gary and I knew taking on a child one year into a new marriage was a risk, but we agreed to stick it out until Samantha turned eighteen...bare minimum. Regardless of the state of "us," the child wouldn't suffer because of it.

Gary worked hard so I could stay home and take care of my health, raise the kids, and pursue whatever path worked for me. In spite of expressed concerns, there was never any other permanent solution to raising Samantha that was considered seriously. She was ours, troubles and all, and we were okay with that. We loved Sammy as our own and treated her as such. In spite of my health, giving up Samantha would have felt like giving up my own child. I couldn't do it. We made it work and Samantha quickly became someone I counted on as a right-hand man. When my children moved out as adults, Samantha became an only child, our only child in the home. With Gary working long hours, it was Sam I hung out with. We shared a love of the same music, watched shows together, shopped together, and became real friends. It was often Sam who helped me with my blood sugar drops, and she quickly became great at detecting when I was having an issue with it, sometimes before I was even aware myself.

I keep up the pacing outside on the deck and light another smoke. I look up at the second-story roofline until the logistics of how she managed to get down from her window begins to nag my thoughts. I had seen Sam swing off the deck to retrieve a fallen shovel one day and had been highly jealous of her skills. She swung like a monkey around the deck railing, lowered herself to the fence railing, skirted along using the deck bench bottom as a hand-hold, and had dropped down to the ground right next to the shovel. She then tossed it up to the deck and reversed the process until she was standing next to me top side once again. The entire process had taken her maybe two minutes. At the time I was impressed; now I was suspicious. But that was from the deck, how would she get down to it?

I walk around looking up at the upstairs roofline, but it's too dark to see anything but the outline. I make a mental note to go back out in the daylight and see how she was getting down. Sam's room doesn't have easy access to the ground. My office sits across the hall from her room and faces the front of the house like hers does. The rooms are mirror images of each other. Even in the case of a fire I would hesitate to jump out my office window, so how had she managed? I come to a complete halt and try to grab hold of the threads that are suddenly bothering me. I can't quite figure out what's under my skin, but I'm pretty sure the answer is in Sam's room. I toss my cigarette butt in the dragon's belly and go back inside. I grab a fresh cup of coffee and head upstairs to Sam's room.

HOUR 2:

She Opted Out...Why?

12:30-1:30 a.m.

Normally I'm a stickler for not breaking room privacy, but Samantha has opted out of this home and I need to know why. I stand at the top of the stairs and look around. I can see all four rooms from this vantage point. The doors are all open and all I see is a whole lot of room that this teen had to call her own. *I would have loved to have had this much space to claim and decorate when I was her age. None of this makes sense. She has a great life.* She has the run of the upstairs, other than my office. With only Samantha left to raise, our five-bedroom home allowed her plenty of space to spread out. She had one room for a hang-out area, her bedroom, her own bathroom, and the guest room all at her disposal. *Most kids would be thrilled with this set-up.* I reach around inside her room to flip the light switch and I'm shocked to find three very large suitcases on the floor.

How was she going to get these huge things out of the house with no one hearing and who in the world do those belong to? It's almost funny and I stand there smirking at the idea that she thought she could ever get these things out of the house at night, with both of us here, without making any noise. Each one was large enough to pack for a two-week trip. *How did these even get into my house without me knowing?!* Was she going to do it *Shawshank Redemption* style? Wait for the trains to pass and toss them out the window as they screech by? I exhale harshly and shake my head. *Even running away wasn't well planned out.* I sit down on the edge of her bed and just take in her room. I look around slowly at the items of her life, breathe in the smells, and close my eyes. *Now what?* The small table at the foot of her bed catches my eye and it's there I find her runaway letter. I don't know why I didn't think to look for one, but seeing it there brings everything to a standstill. The entire room fades but for that one piece of notebook paper, laying face up on the table. The first words catch my eyes...

Dear Mom and Dad

I pick it up, throw a gulp of coffee down my throat, and start to read.

> Dear Mom and Dad
> I'm sorry to do this, but I feel it's best. I need a restart. So I'm leaving. I already have a plan and a place to go. By the [time] you are reading this I won't be in the country. Last week during our fight and you said "Get out of my house" I figured you were right. I know I can make it. I'm sorry I took the money from you that was a very poor choice for me to make. Once I get a job tho I will send you back that money and more, to pay you back. You won't here from me for awhile. My plan is to get my GED. Get a job, start making a living, fix up my life, etc. Once I have done that, I will be in contact. But it still won't happen til I'm at least 20. I feel like this is the right decision. I'm unhappy here and I can't be somewhere where I'm not happy. I know you think sending me to juvie will make me get my shit together. But in all honesty it won't. It will just make everything worse. I need to be on my own. Thats the only way I'll truly be able to learn. I love you both. And I won't ever stop. I'll be in touch when I can. Love, Samantha

Taking a deep breath and a long drink of coffee, I stare at the letter for a few minutes. I wait for the tears to start, but they don't. I'm more confused than anything else. She has a plan and a place to go...where?

Out of the country? How could she do that without a passport or my signature? Learn what? Fix up her life? Was it broken? Why when she's twenty? What was she talking about?! *When did I tell her to get out of my house?!* I read the letter two more times trying to decipher what she means and where she might be headed to or staying. It doesn't make much sense, so I set it aside to look at again later when I get downstairs. *Did I tell her to get out?*

I get back to work finding out why Sam left. *That letter makes no sense. It's like she took parts of our talks and mashed them together.* I recall a conversation last week where after being told for the hundredth time I was unreasonable to expect her to not have F's or skipped assignments I had responded that I was never going to change my expectations; my children would always be expected to go to school and do well; it's their only job as children, but especially as children in this family. Bassett's and Geister's value education, and many of them on both sides are educators. Doing well in school isn't really an option in these families. I told her if she couldn't handle that, then she should find someplace else to live where they had no expectations of behavior or grades. It is as close to an explanation as I can find; and I mull it over while I open each large suitcase and fold the lid back.

Lined up together, open, the large suitcases look like a tornado packed them. Everything is jammed in and unfolded. In the middle of one of the bags is leftovers from the fridge. *Now she has no food. She's out there and she didn't even get to take her leftovers.* My concern for Samantha begins to grow as I find item after item she would need out there to survive. A pocketknife, money, her student ID card. *She is out there with nothing.* The thought sends a chill through me. I find a small notebook with some names and numbers on it that I don't recognize. I set it off to the side and decide to see exactly who my daughter's been associating with over the past few months. *Maybe there's more to her behavior than I thought.* If it's a number, name, or log-in, it goes into a stack for me to go through later. The scraps of paper continue to grow as I find name after name and number after number that I've never seen before. The task gives me something to focus on rather than the thought that my daughter is out there in the night, alone and unprotected. *Sam, where are you?!*

Through her bedroom window I see the lights of the Jeep coming down the street. I race downstairs and press my face to the kitchen door window to watch Gary back up into the carport. I fog up the glass with my breath, so I hold it while he parks. *Is she in there?* I strain to see inside the dark Jeep, but the only door opening is the driver's door. No Sam. My heart sinks like a lead weight. Gary steps out with his head hung low, closes the door, and just stands there. His shoulders heave as he takes in a deep breath and shakes his head back and forth slowly. *He's trying to process this. That poor man. He didn't deserve this Sam. None of us do.*

I turn and pour him a cup of coffee, adding in a little creamer the way he likes it. He walks in and I hand him his cup.

"No sign of her?" I ask.

"None. How could she disappear that quickly? It's a small town and I drove every street, but nothing. How is that even possible?" He takes a long pull on the coffee and looks at me, like he's hopeful I have an answer. I don't.

"Because she's a teenager. If she doesn't want to be found, she won't be. Besides, Sam knows the streets of this town better than we ever will. I'm sure she was slipping around you the whole time."

Sam's Notes-In such a small town I could see Dad coming four blocks away. I would hide behind a bush or a car until he passed by me.

"She just jumped out of her window and took off."

"There's no place to land from her window. It's why I put her in that room. I don't get how she did it."

"She managed. I yelled to her but she just said she had to go, and disappeared. I shouldn't be here drinking coffee. I should be out finding her." His voice is cracking as he fights back the tears. I put his coffee in a bigger to-go cup and he heads out the door, keys and coffee in hand. He's gone before it registers in my mind that he still doesn't have any shoes on.

I can't find my coffee cup so I grab another one, a power bar, and a tote bag, and I head back upstairs to Sam's room for some answers. I stop by my office for a notebook so I can start keeping track of what we do during this journey. I wonder if she's outside somewhere watching the glow come from her bedroom window. I sneak a peek out of my office window to see if I can see her out there in the dark, wanting to come home. I stand there in the dark office, pushing my eyes to take in every blade of grass that's moving. *Is she out there? Is she watching me? Why don't you want to be in here where it's warm, Sam?* There's no movement on the street at all. Even a cat crossing the street would be a welcome sign of life out there. I go back across the hall to her room. *Okay then, let's do this.*

*Sam's Notes-I was watching Mom in my room. I was up the street in the library door opening waiting for my ride. If I pressed up against the south wall, I could pick up on internet. It gave me a chance to change my passwords before Mom found my log-in lists. I knew she would when I saw her in my room. She's like having Judge Judy for a mom. She'll hunt down every lie, ask a million questions, and find every hole in your story. It sucks.

I go to put my coffee down and discover the cold remains of cup #1 on the nightstand. I slide it to the back with my fresh hot cup. I stand chewing the power bar while I survey my target. I'll tackle the bed first so I have a space to work from. Flip the mattress and look and clean underneath. Then there's the suitcases, closet, and dresser. *I've seen enough cop and CSI shows; I've got this.* I run through the list of room targets and prioritize them while I finish my snack. The argument last night had caused me to lose my appetite and I didn't realize how starving I was until I ate that power bar. I toss the wrapper in her overflowing trash can and scoop up her quilt. Between the quilt and the blanket I find a lighter with resin near the tip--signs of her smoking pot. I toss the lighter into my tote and grab the blanket, rolling it into the quilt to make one big ball. I give it a good toss out of her doorway and it lands softly at the foot of the stairs. I grab the sheets and launch another bedding ball down the stairs. Using her bed as a table, I empty the contents of the first suitcase onto it. I toss the ID and phone numbers in my tote with the other numbers I've collected and look at the pile of clothes. Most of them I don't even recognize. I make a pile of clothes to throw down the stairs to be washed. *Good chance to clean before she gets home.*

12:55 a.m. Facebook message received from Paul

"Here's my phone number... Call me as soon as you can." Because I still hadn't turned on my notifications, I didn't receive this message until the morning.

1:15 a.m. Facebook message received from Paul

"You there?"

The mound at the foot of the stairs continues to grow as I make my way through the next two suitcases. I take every item that's not clothing and place it on the bed so I can get a good overall look. Lip gloss, a hairbrush, curling iron, toothpaste but no toothbrush, a notebook but no pen, a flashlight with no batteries in it, some cards from when she was a very young child, and a picture of her cat that had died the previous autumn. She was seeking to bring comfort with her, although not very well planned-out. I pack the items in a duffel bag and place it off to one side of the bed, and take the three suitcases and stack them to one side of the room.

Gary calls to check in. No sign of her. "How could she be gone that quick, Diane? I was out the door maybe two minutes later. She's nowhere to be found."

"Come home, Gary. You won't find her in the dark." My concern for Gary being out there in the dark with no sleep, or shoes for that matter, grows by the minute.

"I just want to check one more area and I'll come back and we'll go from there."

"You could probably use some shoes, too."

"What? Why?"

"Look at your feet, Gary. I'll see you when you get home." I glance at the clock and add up how long he's been awake. He typically leaves the house around 4:30 a.m., drives an hour to work in Portland, works construction for 8-10 hours and then drives home to work on his paperwork until bedtime. *He can't keep this up. He's been up almost twenty-four hours. He HAS to get some sleep.*

I take my cups downstairs and warm the freshest one in the microwave. I get the cabinet fronts wiped down while I think about the runaway letter. It doesn't make any sense to me and I wish Sam were here to ask so she could explain it.

I miss her.

HOUR 3:

Search And Compile

1:30-2:30 a.m.

Gary backs in the driveway and comes inside, head hanging lower than before. He looks like a beaten man. *Damn it, Sam!* I'm angry at her for this. *So you're out partying and we're here, dying. Thanks.* I get him some socks to warm his feet and we sit at the dining room table to discuss where we're at with finding her. It's beginning to feel like a war room. We decide to call the police and get more eyes out there. We live in a very small town, so the chances of finding her before she gets to a bigger city are fairly good--or so we hope. I call the number, but they're closed until morning. We can call the county sheriff if we need immediate assistance, but after some discussion Gary and I opt to wait until morning to give Sam a chance to come home.

"This way if she comes home by morning, no harm no foul, no police involvement."

Gary nods his head in agreement. *He's so tired.*

"Why don't you get some sleep, Gary?"

"I can't sleep. Sam's out there."

"I know, but you've been up almost twenty-four hours and there's no telling how long this could drag out. Sleep now for an hour or two and then I'll catch some later."

Gary reluctantly agrees and heads for the bedroom. He flops down face first on his bed, not even bothering to remove his pants or socks. I leave him where he is, cover him with a blanket, and turn off the bedroom light. I stand there in the doorway and watch him sleeping. The bathroom light is on behind me and the bedroom is lit by the shared light only. His breathing is ragged like when he's overworked himself. It won't be restful sleep for him. I take a deep breath in, hold it, and release it slowly. I do it two more times until I feel a sense of peace rather than nervousness coursing through me. *Focus!* Closing the door softly I take my coffee into the dining room and stand by the window looking out. What a strange night. *What if she's really not coming back?*

I shake my head. *She'll be back any hour.*

I grab some garbage bags, go back upstairs to her room, and prepare to tackle her dresser. I open up the big garbage bags and begin to load in every bit of trash I find, including some slutty-looking underwear I never bought her. Every drawer I open dismays me. Her drawers are complete chaos and I can't help but compare them to the state of her life. *Chaotic room, chaotic life.* There's dirty clothes in the drawers with clean ones, old food, garbage, and some old vapor cigarette cartridges. I examine the vapor cigarette unit and I'm struck by the fanciness of it. *How did a teenager with no job afford this thing?* It's purple glass, engraved, and has to be worth some money. I'm disappointed, and yet oddly relieved she's at least rebelling with her health in mind.

I decide to check her computer. She told me for months that her upstairs computer was used for pictures only because it had no internet access in that room. She claimed she had a program on it that allowed phone chat with friends which is why we would hear her upstairs talking sometimes. I had never followed up on that and checked. *Now seems like a good time.* I'm surprised to find her network drive plugged in the back of her hard drive. *I took that from her months ago and thought I lost it.* I had planned to buy her another when it was time to give her back her upstairs access. *I guess there's no need, the little sneak had it the whole time.* I fire up her desktop and open it up. Most seem like normal things: Word with her school papers, a few movie viewing programs, pictures, videos, and music. I click open the videos and watch only four of over ten videos of her smoking her ecig in her room. *I was downstairs and she was feet above my head making movies of herself smoking?! You have to be kidding me!* I find ones of her with a friend I had strictly forbidden her to be around. The girl was verbally abusive to Samantha and had encouraged sneaky behavior in the past. Since the girl was so much older than Sam—eighteen--I felt justified in squishing the friendship and encouraging Sam to find friends her own age. *I thought she had put that friendship to rest. Obviously not.* Most of the pictures are typical teenager duck-lip selfies, but there are enough that are sexually suggestive that I can't bear to look anymore. *My daughter has been sharing way too much of herself.*

I head back into her bedroom and stand there with my hands on my hips, surveying her space. A cord hanging out from under the bed catches my eye. She's had no phone for a while and I'm confused why she would have a phone charger plugged in if she has no phone to recharge. I examine it and the brand isn't one I recognize. I head back into my office and check the drawer with old phones. I hold up the charger and start comparing it to the phones. I try to plug it in to every old phone, but it doesn't fit any of them. *That girl has a phone, but where did she get it, who's paying for it, and more importantly, what's she doing in exchange for it?!*

Besides a mystery phone charger, I'm also confused by the sheer amount of clothes, make-up, and jewelry that I simply don't recognize. I don't expect to know every item my children have in their rooms, but without a job she shouldn't have this much stuff I don't recognize. *Someone has been providing my daughter a lot of stuff.* I put my back to her wall and just hold still while I look around. She has too much stuff I've never seen, a phone I don't see but she has a charger for, clothes I didn't buy, makeup I didn't provide, internet access she claimed she didn't have, and activities I never approved of. *You've been busy, young lady. I may not have noticed before, Sam, but you sure have my attention now.*

I turn on her closet light and peek inside. *Oh Lord, it's worse than the room!* There's no option but to empty it so I can go through it. I pile everything from her closet onto her floor and start going through each piece of clothing, every backpack and purse. I start checking every pocket and zipper. I'm surprised at how many numbers I recover from her pockets. Quite a few are hidden in clothes that are folded up on a shelf as if they're too small. The pile continues to grow and I toss each new find into the tote bag. I plan to assemble one comprehensive list with every log-in, every name, and every number that I find.

By the time I'm done her dresser is empty and clean, her garbage pile has grown by two bags, and the laundry pile is now creeping up the stairwell. I grab my tote and drinks, turn off her room light, and head downstairs to compile my list of names, numbers, and log-ins, kicking her dirty clothes out of my way as I reach the landing.

I put my tote and cups down, gather up an armful of dirty clothes and head for the basement stairs. I hate going down there, especially at night. I open the door, click on the light, and stand there a minute just listening. In 2014 we learned Samantha had been sneaking men into our basement while we slept, and partying next to my laundry rack of bras and delicates. The loss of privacy and security I felt still hadn't left me, and going downstairs was a daily struggle against the fears that consumed me with every step I descended. The basement had a large closet unit at the foot of the stairs, so when you descended the basement stairs, you were blind to what was on the other side of the closet. Unfortunately, the laundry area was not only down there, it was in the blind area. As much as I wanted never to go down there again once I found out my security and privacy had been violated, getting over it wasn't an option for me. Laundry continues to pile up regardless of fears, so I had continued to just suck it up, run down there fast, and get out as soon as possible! I take a deep breath and start my descent, holding my breath for as long as I can. I rush around the corner to the laundry area but can't keep the air in any longer and exhale, dreading the next moment-the inhale. The smell hits me immediately. *I hate this house. It smells like the pit of hell down here.* I get a load of her clothes started as quickly as I can, with one hand held up to my nose to try and block the stench.

We had cleaned, painted, and searched high and low for the source of the odor in the basement when we first moved in, but could come up with only one strange room under a flight of stairs as a possible explanation. It had ventilation tiles but no purpose nor need for ventilation in an area that was supposed to be a solid block of space. Neither Gary nor I had ever chosen to do more than peer through the ventilation grates and debate the creepiness of the area.

I click "start" on the washer and race around the corner and back up the stairs, not stopping until I'm back on the landing, turning off the light, slamming the door shut, and locking it. That's always my favorite part, when I get to lock the door. I rest my back against it and exhale slowly. I made it.

I stop by the kitchen to stare into the fridge. I feel like I should eat to soak up some of the coffee that's now ripping apart my insides. Nothing looks appealing, so I grab a piece of bread from the bread bag and eat it untoasted. It's as good as anything else right now. At least it's food.

I sit down at the table with my tote of numbers and start going through what I've found. Taking my notebook, I rip out two pages, one for known contacts and one for unknowns. It doesn't take me long to have the two lists compiled. I look at the unknown names and numbers and cross-reference the numbers to all other information I gathered. Have I found any notes with that name or number on it, is there any mention of these names in any of the messages I had found, do any of her doctors or homeschool network have that number? Eventually I get the list of unknowns down to about ten names I can't identify. I take those names and do Google and Facebook searches for each one. I look at their pictures to see if I recognize the backgrounds, I look at their friends lists to see if I recognize any of their contacts. Doing this eliminates a couple more names from the list as people from school she didn't have much contact with. I pull her last cell phone bill out that I still have and compare the names and numbers to her call list, and by doing this I come up with four names that are listed too many times to be a coincidence. Using Reverse Phone Number search I trace the numbers back to the registered owners. As is usual, the only information the site will give me is an approximate location of the owner of that number within about a two block radius. It's enough. I print up a map of the areas shown and mark off where the phone area is considered to be. When I'm done, we have four good locations to go search.

I stack the map and lists together to show Gary later, do some picking up, and go sit in the family room. The kitchen and dining room lights are on, so it's backlit and peaceful in here. A train screeches past and I'm reminded how irritating living here has been. *I've had to take two trips this year just to get some rest and peace. No wonder Sam has asked us multiple times to move this past year.* We should have listened. An idea begins to sprout in my brain.

HOUR 4:
An Overdue Talk

2:30-3:30 a.m.

I check in on Gary and he's snoring deeply. At least he's getting some kind of rest. Quietly unlocking the patio doors, I slip outside in the chilly early morning air. The back deck looks out over a river, a marina, and a wildlife refuge. It was supposed to be a place we could stay until Sam graduated. *It looks like a Norman Rockwell painting. Sam, why couldn't you ever fit in here?* My head hurts. I rub my forehead and look out over the deck to the dark world beyond. The lamps in the marina parking lot stand out and glow like soft little orbs of gold floating in the mist. I stand there in the dark, close my eyes, and pray. *Lord, I'm begging you. I'm begging you, please keep her safe and warm tonight.* I try to think of more to pray, but can't. I just stand there in the dark, hands clutched in a prayer that no longer needs words. I just open my heart to Him and let Him feel my pain, and I cry. I stand there in the dark, my cheeks streaked with tears, palms up, and I beg Him for a shred of grace. I stand that way for a minute, then slowly peek through one open eye. *Do I stand here until you answer me orrrr...? Would I know what grace looks like?* I drop my hands. *I have GOT to learn how to do this prayer thing! Is it head up, hands up...or hands folded head bowed...?* I wish I could call my friend and Bible study partner up for advice, but it's far too late back East to wake D.W. up. I head back inside and lock up. *She might need to get back in.* I go back and unlock the door, then turn to head up the stairs to her room. *She opted out.* I turn back and lock the door, and turn once again to head upstairs. *She might want in.* I turn back and unlock the door, leaving my hand on the lock. *Make up your mind. Locked or unlocked? Unlocked. It's cold out tonight. Did she take her coat? Is she safe?*

I'm losing it.

Later, maybe. Not now.

I'm so tired. I just want to sleep and not wake up until this is all over. I glance at my watch and can't believe it's been only a few hours. *Everything was okay just hours ago.*

Gary wakes up and wanders out into the living room. He stares at me with that blank stare that people have when their brain is still asleep and they're not sure why you're standing there looking at them. I stare back, too tired to tell him he woke up. We stand there like two zombies in a staring contest until a train goes by down near the waterfront. We both take in a deep breath and sit at the table, as if by instinct now.

"You look beat; you need to sleep," Gary tells me.

"I know, but I wanted to get some stuff done. Now that you're up, I'd like to talk when you're awake enough to hold a conversation."

"Let me splash some water on my face and I'll be right back." Gary heads for the bathroom and I assemble the stack of lists and map like a business presentation. There have been a few things nagging me and I want to make sure we are on the same page and communicating.

Gary comes back and sits down. "What a night, right?"

"It has been, and it's not over, sadly. I was wondering about something you said earlier. You said you saw her jump and called out to her...?"

"Yeah, I was on the stairs because I figured she'd jump. When I heard her window open I ran into her room but she had just landed on the ground. She had her skateboard with her and she just stopped and said, 'Sorry Dad, I have to go,' and just like that she was gone."

"Why would you figure she would jump?" *That's a strange thing to assume.*

"Because when I was in her room earlier I saw the suitcases and letter and I talked to her about it. She promised me she wasn't going to run away, though." As soon as the word "earlier" hit the air, I begin to have a problem with his account of the evening.

"You're telling me you had a conversation with Samantha tonight, in her room, you knew about the suitcases and letter and yet you didn't think telling me was a good idea because...?!" I feel my anger rising as the missed opportunity for getting through to her hits me, and the possible consequences of his choice not to share it with me in time sink in.

"I had it under control--well, at least I thought I did. We talked, she said she wouldn't run away, she told me she loves me and was really tired and just wanted to go to sleep."

I'm trying so hard not to turn this into a finger-pointing argument, so I hold all comments, which for me is very difficult. But inside my head, there is a lot of finger-wagging, head-shaking, foot-stomping, and nagging going on. *You should have told me, Gary.*

"Is this why you were on the stairs when I came out for water?" The night's events begin to fall into place a bit more.

"Yeah. I didn't believe her when she said she wouldn't run away tonight, so I thought I should hang out and just wait, watch."

"And when I walked by to get my water, still no need to tell me?"

"No, I probably should have."

Lesson Learned: Don't ever have to mutter the words "I probably should have." Not where your child's safety is concerned. Go with your gut and share any and all information with the other adults in the child's network if you sense or see that a change of circumstances is happening. Even if you feel you have it under control, you still need to share the knowledge.

A million snide comments roll through my brain too fast to distinguish them from each other. I lock my lips together as if held there with glue to keep from turning this into an argument about our communication problem. I take a few deep breaths through my nose to steady my anger.

"Did you see her jump? I'm confused how she did it." I still need information, so I'm forced to press on with questions when so far I haven't liked many answers.

"I heard the window open, ran up the stairs, and was in her room in time to see her standing up after landing on the ground."

"Was she hurt or injured from it that you could see?"

"No, she looked fine. She had her skateboard and ripstik with her. She just took off and disappeared."

We discuss how we think she planned to get her big suitcases out of the house without us hearing the commotion, and agree she was probably going to throw them out the window, but didn't have time when he wouldn't leave the stairwell.

*Sam's Notes—Actually, I was planning to take them down one at a time when the trains passed, slipping them out onto the back deck and then coming back inside for the next bag. It would have taken me three trips and three trains, but I was pretty sure it would work. Dad hanging out on the stairs blew that plan, though, so I just left them behind.

A thought hits me and I ask Gary, "Have you been going out back on the deck before bed lately?"

"Why would I do that? The mosquitoes eat me alive."

"Because recently I've been finding the patio door unlocked when I get up to get water in the middle of the night. I figured it was you forgetting to lock it when you came back in. I don't know, I thought maybe you were taking in the view before bed."

"Nope, not me. Do you think that's how she's been getting in and out?"

"I'm guessing so, but then what was she doing on the nights I was finding it unlocked and locked it up before I went to bed?"

We talk some more about the different ways she could have been getting in and out of the house without us finding out, and agree it's not that hard if she wanted to.

Gary asks me, "Have you seen the ladder upstairs on the roof of the carport?"

"What ladder?" *I swear I'm going to scream if there's a ladder up there and he never said a word about it. But then, I never mentioned the unlocked door to him.*

"When I was cleaning the gutters I saw an old ladder on the upper roof over the carport. It looks old, though; I doubt she's been using it." *He doubts she's been using it?!* I physically jam my lips together to prevent a snide comment from escaping. *Getting mad at him isn't helping.*

I take a deep breath and focus on the goal: information that brings Samantha home, not who was more innocent or more guilty. *We both failed her.* "I've never seen it, but will you show it to me when it's light out? Is it stored in a place where it could be used?

"It's over the carport up against the wall. I'll show you tomorrow. She'd be nuts to use it, though; it's old."

*Sam's Notes--They were close, but not quite. I tried to use that ladder once; it was gross and old. I discovered I didn't need it. Mom parked her Jeep in the carport with the bumper hanging out. It was pretty simple to climb out the bathroom window during a train, walk over to the carport roof, and then swing down onto her Jeep. I got back in by climbing back on top of it and swinging up to the carport roof. I could also swing down onto the deck railing, walk across the top of it, and then drop down onto the deck. Or even easier was get down to the basement and just go out the door, leaving it open or closing it and using the dog door to get back in. I also used Kleenex wadded up in the door locks so it looked closed and locked but could be pulled open when I needed to. There were a bunch of ways in and out, to be honest.

I talk to Gary about what's been happening with her schoolwork. The struggles with getting her up, her refusal to work on any papers in front of me, claiming I made her nervous, and her failing grades and piss-poor attitude.

"Why didn't you say anything about it before now?"

"Truly I don't think you should ask me that question, Gary, given where we are tonight." My ability not to get angry over his knowledge before she jumped is simmering below a very tired surface. It would only take one comment that I found to be offensive for this to blow up, and questioning my lack of open communication is pushing my limits of mouth control. Again I lock my lips shut and rub my forehead.

"Stop." His one-word response jars my thoughts.

"What?"

"Leave your forehead alone, Diane; you're rubbing it raw."

I hit the mirror app on my iPad and see he's right; I've worn a red streak straight across my forehead. It's a nervous habit to rub my forehead, and as I've done in the past, when really stressed, I rub it more than it can handle. It's sticky and close to bleeding. I take a napkin off the holder in the middle of the table and dab at the stickiness. The napkin sticks to the wound and tears so I'm left with little wisps of napkin stuck to my forehead. *I'm lovely.* I toss the shredded napkin in the trash and try to ignore the bits stuck to me.

I show Gary the list of names and my map of target areas from the reverse phone number search. He's notably impressed with my work while he caught a little sleep.

"Nice work. Do you want me to head down and check the neighborhoods out?"

"No, not alone. I want to be there so we can scope the places out. You'll need to drive; I'll snoop. The maps give only general neighborhood locations, not addresses, so let me do some more searching later to see if I can narrow down the search zone by digging out some addresses, get a few pictures off of social media of what their house looks like, and use Zillow and Google Maps to zero in on the targets without cruising whole neighborhoods."

"Cool. Let me know if you need my help doing that. I wouldn't mind learning how you do that search stuff you do on people. It's too dark now, but let's hit that tomorrow and see what we can find."

HOUR 5:

A Pleading Post...

3:30-4:30 a.m.

Gary decides to get one more drive around town in before sunrise and insists I lie down. I can barely keep my eyes open, it's hard to focus, and I feel weak. I agree even though I doubt sleep will come.

I lie down on my bed and he comes in, putting my blanket over me.

"I want you to stay down, promise me. Just for an hour if you can't fall asleep, but at least let your body rest for an hour."

"Big advice coming from the 24-hour man, but okay."

"Yeah, well...24-hour man laid down for a few hours, and so far you haven't."

I give him the required comforting words and snuggle into my pillow, closing my eyes and sighing heavily. I mummer a goodbye and wait to hear the door close. I open my eyes and start to sit up but he pops the door open.

"I'm serious, Diane. You're diabetic. Rest." He smiles because he busted me, but I know he's right. It was nice snuggled down in the pillow for those few seconds. I again snuggle in and reassure him I'll stay down. Again I hear the door close, but this time I remain snuggled in.

The door closes again softly and I listen as his footsteps head out to the hall. They stop, come back, and again I hear the door softly open and close, and the footsteps walking normally out to the kitchen. The squeak of the kitchen door and the sound of the Jeep tells me he's on his way and I pop out of bed and race to the window to sneak a peek out of the curtain corner. I watch as the Jeep swings onto Mill Street and heads east.

I return to the dining room and survey the papers and maps. I just know I can narrow down those targets to an actual address. A huge yawn escapes me and I'm aware my head is swimming. I go back in and stand by my bed, debating the pros and cons of sleep. *The diabetes votes yes. The mom votes no. The eyes vote yes. The heart votes no.* I sit down on the edge of the bed to continue the debate with myself about staying up. *How can I sleep when I don't where she is? How can you find her if you don't?* That logic shuts up my thoughts and guilty feelings and I wrap my big white thermal blanket around myself to ward off the chilly morning air. Gary and I sleep with the window open all winter, preferring fresh cold air to stuffed or canned moderate air. I wrap the thermal around myself and sit on the edge of my bed looking out to Mill Street. I'm aware I'm exhausted, but my head won't lie back on the pillow. I keep trying and I keep sitting up. *Mom's guilt. You can't sleep, you know you can't. You need to think, not sleep.* I settle on propping up the pile of pillows behind me clear up to my neck so my head's on the pillows, but I'm still sitting upright. I can close my eyes and rest them while still letting my brain run free with everything I had learned. *I have to admit it feels good to sit still in the dark and snuggle under the blanket.* It brings me a little comfort and I curl it under my chin with my fist like I'm an infant. I may think like a warrior, but it doesn't mean I don't like to be comforted while I do it.

As I lay there I go over the events in my head. Our fight over the ATM money taken, Gary's reaction to it, and the words I spoke that led her to jump. *She prepped to jump, he caught her, talked to her, she makes a fake agreement with him, and then she leaps. There's the strange runaway note, the unknown clothes and make-up. The unfamiliar names. The log ins. The log-ins! I never checked the log-ins!*

I toss the thermal blanket to the side, jump up, and run to the dining room to grab the pile of names and information. I come back into my bedroom, wrap the thermal blanket around myself, sit back down on my bed, and open up my iPad. I shuffle the lists until I find the log-in list. If I hurry I can screenshot everything she's said, when, to whom, and figure out what's going on, and where she disappeared to. I have to download a few of the apps as I don't typically have teenager chat rooms loaded on my devices. *I feel like a pervert downloading teen chat sites!* I start attempting to log into her accounts. One website and app after another informs me the passwords have been changed in the past few hours. I'm able to log into one for a few seconds, but I'm booted off almost immediately. When I attempt to log back in, that password has been changed as well. Even though I'm unable to access any of her accounts, in a strange way I find comfort in this; I know she's still out there. She's somewhere she can access the internet this very minute. Oddly this website has just provided me with a glimmer of hope she's okay. I smile just a little. It's a ray of light, and I'm desperate for any light whatsoever.

Lesson Learned: Collect those log-ins and use them immediately before they can change the passwords. The second you log in, change the password yourself. That way even if they try to log in while you are still on the site, they won't have access. As soon as you have the password changed, quickly switch the registered email to your own. This eliminates any ability they have to have a new password sent to their email. Once in the account, take a screen shot of everything (holding the power and home button down at the same time on a device typically clicks a picture of your screen, called a screenshot). It's your resource for dates, times, names, numbers and so much more. The screenshot will be saved as a picture in your pictures file.

Any scan through of runaway stories, or missing children reports on TV, typically include pleas from the parents, so I decide to plead to Samantha.

I message Samantha's Facebook account a begging plea. "Please, Boo, contact us. Please. Tell us what's going on. We can't help you if we don't know what's going on. My heart is breaking into pieces. We'll come get you wherever you are, no questions asked. Just don't leave us not knowing where our child is. We are dying here, please Sammy. Please!" I doubt it will get a response from her, but I can hope she at least sees it. I can hope she's one of the ones who claim the pleas matter.

<u>Sam's Notes:</u> Mom killed me with that message. I almost went home when I read it. Almost. It was hard to read though, and I looked at it a few times while I was gone. I hated hurting her and Dad. I just didn't know what else to do.

I lie back on the pillow mound, cover myself with the blanket and close my eyes for a few minutes. *I simply can't hold them open any longer.* I drop into a complete dark void of time until the neighbor's dog barking wakes me up half an hour later.

HOUR 6:

Street Name Winco

4:30-5:30 a.m.

I wake with my own words ringing in my ears: "Sam, get out of my house--I can't take your drama anymore!"

She was right, I HAD said it. Last week. The horror that I had indeed spoken those words to her sinks my heart and I sit up on the bed and just stare at the floor. *I'm horrible.* Tears begin to fall from my eyes as I recall the explosive argument last week that had led to those words being spoken to her.

The chief of police had called me. Officer Harris had found Samantha and her best friend Carla in a neighborhood near the school. A neighbor had called them in because the girls were staggering around the homes as if drunk. Carla had started throwing up in a lady's front yard and the police had been alerted. At the time Sam was supposed to be at a Speech and a Debate meeting to determine if she enjoyed it enough to join. The police chief let me know she had also responded and breathalyzer tested the girls; they passed, so she had returned them to the high school. She had gotten a weird feeling about them, though, and had parked and followed them in to the school, where she observed them sneaking around the corner of the gym to go smoke. She again hauled them back to Speech and Debate. Sam had called her dad and I listened as she told him all about how great S & D was and how she might like to join. I was in the middle of telling Gary about the call from the police chief when Sam called him with her tales of interest in the program. I had stopped her claims, told her the police chief had just called me, and to wait at the school for her dad to come pick her up. She had come in the house with a horrendous attitude, and to make it worse Gary had stood just behind her facing me. I felt it was two on one as I battled her to admit she had made a poor choice by leaving the school grounds and lying about the meeting. Gary had argued she hadn't done anything too out of bounds, she had smirked in my direction, and I had lost my cool. I had yelled at her to just get out of my house because I couldn't take her drama anymore, and stomped off. We had talked about it shortly afterwards, and she told me she knew I was just mad and that she didn't take me seriously. I believed her when I shouldn't have. She remembered, and she wasn't over it.

I look at my watch and note I only slept half an hour. *Not enough, but enough for now.* I grab a bottle of water and check my Facebook. I do a quick check and look at my messages. I see there's "other" messages, meaning messages from people I don't know. Normally I leave them alone and don't check them. They're usually sexual contact invites from strangers living in Kenya, which I delete unread. I'm pretty sure I'm on a list somewhere, I get so many. However, given our night I click on the folder marked "other" and find a message from Paul, father to one of Sam's friends, insisting it's urgent he talk to me. He has information. I look at my watch and debate calling a stranger at this hour. Gary returns quiet and sad. I tell him about the message and we decide to call the man in spite of the hour.

What ensues changes our "truth" about Sam, and sets our course for finding her. His information takes us from a misbehaving teenager out there partying to a potential sex trafficking incident.

4:48 a.m. Facebook message response to Paul

"We're here"

We sit and stare at the screen and wait for a response. Gary doesn't operate a Facebook account so I spend a minute explaining how we will be able to tell when Paul is back online. The minutes drag slowly.

"Let's just risk it and call him, Gary. He says it's urgent. If he didn't want to be woken up, he should have said 'when you get around to it.' Let's call him."

Our phones are about out of battery power so we plug them into the wall socket and settle our backs up against the living room wall. We sit there in silence, side-by-side on the carpet, staring out the living room window. *We make a sad sight.*

5:09 a.m. Facebook message response to Paul

"Gary will be calling you from his work phone in a few minutes. I hope we won't be waking you, but you said it was urgent."

Gary enters the number but before he hits call, he and I look at each other in the eyes. It's like we sense this call is about to change everything. I grab a notebook and pen and we brace ourselves. Gary hits "call" and puts us on speaker.

"Hello Paul, this is Diane. You left me a message about my missing daughter Sam. I'm sorry for the middle-of-the-night call, but you said you have information...." *I never thought I'd be the parent making these calls.* Paul is happy to hear from me and shares his own story about his daughter Mary running away a couple of months ago. He's been tracking his daughter through her phone and wonders if we can do that with Sam's. We aren't able to because we just found out she even has a phone. We certainly don't have the number, much less an ability to track it.

"Well, that's too bad, it's made it nice to see where Mary has been the past few months."

Months?! "We're hoping Sam won't be out on the streets that long. We figure she'll be home by morning."

Paul gives a little snort that I pick up on. It's unsettling, as if he knows what we have yet to learn: You don't get them back in a day.

He tells us about the texts between Sam and Mary and his concerns with what he's been reading.

"Do you know Samantha has a street name?"

"No" Gary and I look at each other skeptically. *Who is this man and what's he talking about a street name?!*

"It's Winco because she hangs out behind the Winco store."

A small sounds escapes my mouth, like a small snort of a laugh. Winco? The cheapest food store around? *I wouldn't even be their customer at night, much less hang out behind their store!* Robberies at local Wincos as customers haul their carts of food to their cars seems to be a regular newspaper crime report entry. We even discussed the safety of the different Wincos in my criminal justice studies; it's that bad there. To hear my child carries the street name of THAT store is embarrassing.

"When is she doing that? I know where Sam is from morning until night." I jot on my notebook and hold it up for Gary to see: "This guy is nuts." Gary looks at the phone and rolls his eyes. He takes the pen and scribbles "Winco?! Lol." I smile, take the paper, and get ready to write the next comment. Paul's next statement halts the pen in mid-air.

"According to the texts between the girls it's almost every night after you go to sleep. She's staying out until right before her dad goes to work and right before homeschool."

As much as I'd like to believe he's delusional, his story has enough plausibility to it to freeze me in my defense of Sam and cause me to drop the pen to the floor. *It could be--think about it.* The back door I'd find unlocked, her constant state of being exhausted, or the way she could swing around the deck. Gary and I look at each other and grow quiet as we begin to show this stranger some respect. He clearly knows things about our daughter even we don't, and if we want to get her back, the time to shut up, listen, and take notes had just begun. I pick the pen back up and prepare to learn about my daughter.

"So she's been sneaking out and going down to the Winco store at night? Do the texts say why she's hanging out down there?"

Paul hesitates. He hesitates far too long. As each second of silence drags out, my heart races a bit more.

He clears his throat and seems to be hunting for just the right words to use. "That's where she meets her...man, I really hate to just be sharing these things with you like this. Maybe we should meet up."

"Paul, we need to find Sam. Just tell us, it's okay." *I lie. It's not okay; I don't think I'm going to like what you're about to say.*

"The Winco is where she meets her customers." That last word hangs in the air between the phones.

Customers. Customers. Behind a Winco? Reality snakes around my heart like barbed wire fencing and began to squeeze. I look down fully expecting to see blood coming from my chest wall. Instead I stare into the face of the most hurt man I've ever seen. Gary has huge blue eyes, but right now they're sinking into his skull and losing their shine. They are filling with tears that don't fall, just pool up.

"Wait, customers? What customers?" Maybe we had misunderstood him, maybe he meant something else. *What else could he have meant?*

Again Paul takes too long to answer. He takes a deep breath, loud enough for us to hear him on speaker phone. "This is really hard for me to tell you." *Hard for us to hear.* "Sam has been associating with a known pimp for a while now. Sex trafficking. She told Mary she was being tried out tonight and if she's good enough, she's being sold to two men. I'm so sorry."

Sex trafficking?

Sold. To two men?!

NO! I shake my head to clear his words out, but they cling like peanut butter. My child was out there, being "tried out" so she could be sold?! Paul continues to talk--about his daughter, his plans for a support group, and the months he has been going through this. *Months.* Again the word NO floated through my thoughts. *No.* We're not doing months of this, and my daughter is not property to be bought and sold. *NO!* I screamed that word in my head over and over again.

I stare at Gary as the tears quietly roll down my cheeks. He stares back at me with a look of pure pain in his eyes. His eyes no longer have pooled tears; they are flowing down his face freely. We just sit there, staring at each other with tears streaming while this stranger tells us horrid things about our daughter and her secret night life over the past few months.

"Are you aware she goes to parties regularly?"

"No. We see her in bed, we go to bed. We wake up, she's here."

Please quit asking us if we're aware. We're not aware of anything, obviously. Just assume we suck and save yourself the question.

"Her messages reveal she's been sneaking out almost every night, and meeting up with this guy Higgs, the pimp."

The name rings a bell from the list I compiled and my stomach turns. His name was with her school friends, his name looked like any other name. I don't know if I expected a pimp's name to be something more obvious, but I didn't expect it to blend in with every other name on a contact list.

"So you're telling us our daughter has a pimp, Higgs, and that she sneaks out regularly and parties. Is there anything else?" *Please don't let there be more.*

"Well, most concerning is the arrangement for later with the two men."

"Yes, that is most concerning. That meeting can't happen. Is the Winco being discussed the one in your town, or Vancouver?"

"The Winco in Hazel Dell by Hwy 99 and 99th Street."

I circle the Winco on the target map and put a #1 next to it and hold it up for Gary to see. He takes the pen and underlines it with !!! after it. *Our daughter will NOT be a street hooker. I don't care who thinks they own her!*

"There's also the drinking and drug use she admits to in the texts." I think at least five hairs just went gray. I start to rub my forehead but the wisps of napkin dropping onto my lap remind me to stop.

"What drugs?"

"Looks like pot, alcohol, ecstasy, coke, and molly."

"What's molly?" I've taken courses in drugs and drug counseling; I had never heard the term molly before.

"And did you know she regularly sleeps in the park?"

As grateful as I am for the information, I begin to hit my overload point. "Now you're saying our child lives likes she's homeless? That makes no sense. She has three rooms to use here--why be on the streets?"

"She says she sleeps in your local park and uses the fire station to clean up in."

I recall walking through town with Sam one day. I mentioned I needed to get home to use the bathroom and she responded by pointing at the firehouse. "You can use theirs, Momma. It's always open." I had responded about my dislike of public restrooms and we had continued on, but now that conversation came back to me with meaning. *I'm so stupid. How did I not see?*

"I'll get you copies of those texts and messages." He never forwarded them, and to date I've never actually seen any of them.

"Don't tell Mary anything. I think she forgets I can track her messages. I don't want to put it in her face that I know where she's been and what she texts." I reassure him that of course we won't.

"You should come over later, bring any names you have and I can fill you in on who's who." We don't ever make it over there; we don't need to. We have her back before a meeting is needed.

I just sit there, mind flipping back and forth between blank and reeling. *Sam's being sold. What do I do right this minute to fix this?* The realization I'm helpless floods over me like a cold, dark river. For a moment I want to let it carry me away, just give in to it and sink to the floor into the pool of blackness that welcomes me. I'm aware my heart is racing and feels like it's made of lead. *This is actual physical pain. She's going to kill me. I won't make it through this one.*

HOUR 7:

Facing Reality Without Throwing Up

5:30-6:30 a.m.

The call with Paul continues. He's a wealth of information on Sam's activities for the past six months.

Paul attempts to soften the blows of his phone call by discussing his issues with his daughter Mary. I'm so distracted by what he's told us, though; nothing he says gets farther than my outer ear where it feels like an annoying mosquito. I want to tell him to shut up, to take it all back, to go away and cease to exist. *You've shattered my view of my girl, our lives. Who are you?!*

He tells us he has after care lined up for Mary if she ever comes back. Drug rehabilitation and mental health counseling. He advices us to start looking at her after care plan for when we find her.

"Check your insurance company. They should be able to advise you on what Sam qualifies for."

"Has Mary agreed to go to rehab if she comes back?"

"She's actually a bit excited to go. It's what we talk to her about, her need to get things figured out, to get herself where she wants to be in life."

I make a note to start the after-care process. It's hard to want to line that up when I don't know if Sam's alive, sold, gone... dead?

The tears continue to flow freely and quietly down both our cheeks as this strange man drones on and on about his troubled daughter. I wish he had told us this before we let the girls develop their friendship. If I had known this friend of Sam's had issues, I would have limited their friendship. *Or did that lead to the problem-- limiting her friends?* Or was it not getting to know the moms and dads of her friends well enough? These girls had been friends almost a year and yet this was my first conversation with Paul. Another pang of guilt hits me.

We end the call, and sit in stunned silence against the living room wall. My body begins to convulse involuntarily. I clench my fists into the carpet and will myself to remain calm. My stomach flips and twists. I burp what tastes and smells like stomach acid. Neither one of us wants to be the one to break the silence, but the groans that begin to emit from my throat break the ice. I clamp my hand over my mouth and stare at Gary wide-eyed and desperate. I try to gulp in some air, but none goes down. The hand over my mouth begins to shake uncontrollably and Gary reaches for me. A scream comes from me that I've never heard before and Gary grabs hold of me, pulling me into him. I collapse against his chest in anguish as he wraps around me in his own pain.

"They're trying her out? She's being sold tonight? Gary no, no, no." I keep screaming until the vomit begins to rise in my throat. I break free, run for the bathroom and kneel over the toilet bowl. My throat is convulsing, gagging for air, and dry heaving. Gary stands in the doorway looking concerned, his face soaked in his tears. I beg my own self to pass out and not wake until this is over. My self denies myself and I'm forced to sit there crouched over a toilet, that quite frankly now that I'm eye level with it I'm wishing I had cleaned it today. The sight of that dirty toilet rim looking at me is just the face slap I need. I sit back and wipe my eyes. *That's just gross. I need to clean that.* I sniff and stand up, and turn the cold water on in the sink. I let it fill my cupped palms and sink my face into the icy water. *Trying her out.* I gag, so I release the water and fill my hands up, plunging my face down into the icy water again. *They're selling her.* I feel the bile rise and I release the water and refill my hands, plunging my face back into the ice cold water. I do this over and over again until my stomach stops trying to revolt against the information and my eyes stop feeling the size of golf balls. I stare at my Rudolph reflection in the bathroom mirror. *This sucks. This sucks.*

We walk to the dining room table in complete silence. I wipe my eyes and stare down at the table. Each of us has Paul's information rolling through our brains. Minutes tick by with just the two of us at the table, coffee cups being held more for warmth than the liquid inside, staring at the table top. Finally our eyes lock and we exhale together, and I start to cry again. "Our daughter's a hooker?!" The words escape my mouth before I know they are there. The look on Gary's face says he had the same thought. He hangs his head and rubs his brow. "I need to go find her, Diane. But I'll tell you this--if I find her in a car with men; I'll be in jail. I'll kill them, I'll rip their heads off and wipe the pavement with their bodies. No one will be able to stop me, you know."

"I know. I'd do the same."

"I won't be able to stop once I start. I will literally stomp them into the ground."

"I know. I'm not asking you to stop. Keep stomping until they can't do this again."

Gary takes a long deep breath and I hear it shake as he exhales. He's barely holding it all in. If he comes across these guys, I have zero doubt he'll rip them limb from limb. "I suppose I had better get going. I'll need to let the guys know I won't be in when I get back. I won't be long; I just want to check the town one more time. I'll be back in a few minutes. Later I'm going to make a long trip around every Winco parking lot, starting with 99th & 99th, when it gets later. When the pigs come out, apparently."

"Right?! I can't believe that goes on in their parking lot. That's crazy. It has to be at night--they're too busy in the daytime to have that going on. In the meantime, though, I'll email Sue who lives down by that Winco and have her check the parking lot. It's too far to drive to be taking stabs in the dark with locating her. Let me get eyes that are close enough to keep watch going on that store."

"Sounds good. I'll be back."

I lock up behind him and as I turn I catch my reflection in the mirror. I look distraught and tired. *You're the mother of a missing child. You're the mother of a young lady out there being tried out and sold.* The words hurt.

I'll cry someday in September when I have time.

I drop Sue a quick email asking her to check the 99th & 99th Winco for Sam, to call me if she sees her around the parking lot. I don't want to make it public yet, but Sue lives blocks away and can keep watch easier than we can. Knowing she's elderly and not on social media I trust her to just quietly check and let me know if she sees anything. I ask her not to approach Sam, but instead to call me immediately.

I pass by the sink and see her glass from last night sitting there. It's just a glass, and yet the sight of it makes my eyes fill with tears. *Will I ever see another dirty dish from her again? How many times have I grumbled about her leaving dirty dishes in the sink? I'd give anything to have another dirty dish from her.* I keep busy by loading the dishwasher with leftover containers from the fridge, but I can't bring myself to load her glass. I run my hand over the glass and hold it, hoping to feel her essence through the object. Of course I can't, but the act of trying brings me a small dose of comfort. My hand is where hers was just hours ago, when she was still my little girl. *Those days are gone now.* I put it on the counter behind the coffee maker, although I'm not sure why. It just seems wrong to wash the last dish she used.

I sit by the sun porch windows and look out over the river. The sun is just rising and everything looks so calm and peaceful...out there. *What's so wrong with this place, Sam? Why couldn't you just make it work here?* I take some deep breaths and allow the hot coffee to slip slowly down my throat, enjoying the warmth it provides. *It was a cold night--I wonder if she was warm. They tried her out.* The words jolt my tired brain back to reality once again, and I get up to brush my teeth and freshen up. *They tried her out.* This time the words cause my coffee to rise in my throat and I fight the urge to vomit. I brush my teeth and sit down on the edge of the tub, needing something to support me while I calm my spinning head. *She could be sold by now. Sold or dead.*

I wander from room to room hoping to find an answer in the air. *She hates it here.* A train goes by and screams out its presence with every screeching turn of the metal wheels. I walk up to Sam's room and sit there listening to the train. It's much louder up here. *That's worse, if that's even possible.* I feel bad she had to live with that annoyance. The walls shake, the windows rattle, and a fine layer of dust filters through everything. The train passes and the quiet, beautiful, early-morning sounds return, only to be shattered less than a minute later by a train traveling in the opposite direction.

Gary returns--no sign of her in town.

6:00 a.m. Facebook message received from Paul

Mary headed to Battleground according to phone tracker.

Gary is right there and immediately grabs his keys and prepares to head to Battleground. It's a twenty-minute drive, but we're hopeful she's traveling with Mary and Gary can intercept her as she gets into town.

"Is it worth driving over there when we don't know where she'll be?"

"It's better than sitting here doing nothing, Diane. I'm going nuts. I'd rather be out driving around with a chance of spotting her."

"Keep your phone up and on loud and I'll call if I get a lead."

"You call me with any leads whatsoever and I'll follow up on them."

We get him packed up with a power bar and more coffee and send him out the door. He has acid reflux and needs to stop and take a pill before leaving. All the coffee is ripping his insides apart--as if the missing child wasn't enough to handle that job. He pops his pill, grabs his stuff, and heads out the door with a "Call me for any reason." I wave a hand in acknowledgement and close the door. Leaving my hand on the jamb I lean forward and rest my forehead against the cool exterior door. It's been such a long night and I'm so tired.

Gary calls later--no sign of her. I plead with him to come home. There's nothing to be done without better leads.

6:28 a.m Email from Sue

"Checked Winco, no sign of her. Will check again until she's home."

I go to Sam's room to wait for Gary to come down the street. He's so exhausted. I bow my head and start to pray. I pray for her safety, for his, for my heart not to break, for my thoughts to stay focused on getting her safe. I give in and allow myself a few minutes to cry, sitting on her bed, holding her blanket, rocking back and forth. But crying won't keep her out of their hands. Information will.

HOUR 8:

Plan Of Attack

6:30-7:30 a.m.

We need to move. She's always hated this house and this town, and if we ever find her, we're moving. *I might as well pack as I sort.* Moving had been discussed ever since our first morning in this house when the romantic notion of trains nearby gave way to the stark reality that when you live near train tracks, your life and sleep are shattered every few minutes by their noise. When the trains weren't running, we lived in the middle of a country postcard-- the river view and the wildlife refuge, with its varities of wildlife and birds to enjoy watching through binoculars. Without the trains I could live here happily the rest of my life. But the trains just wouldn't stop, and the noise wouldn't stop, and the coal dust wouldn't stop flying everywhere; it made it impossible to live life in peace.

And then there's the problem with the house. All of us walked around claiming the house just "wasn't right." You couldn't avoid it. On two occasions I saw a man in black that disappeared as soon as I looked at him. Then there was the water bottle incident. I went upstairs to my office one day and put my things down. When I turned to go back downstairs for something I had forgotten, there was an empty water bottle sitting in the doorway I had just walked through. Not only could it not have been there unnoticed when I walked in, I would have knocked it over walking past it when I entered. I stared at the bottle in confusion. The bottle fell over, made three turns, and rolled off to the wall by Sam's room. I loudly stated as I walked down the stairs, "I don't see you. I don't acknowledge you. I have good rent here, so I don't see you. I'm not leaving until I'm ready. Nope. Nope." I had continued with my business but always felt watched when I was upstairs.

My daughter Kate stayed with us for a week and she said she wouldn't come back until we moved. Her guest room door had opened and shut repeatedly during the night, so she had gotten up and latched it closed. A few minutes later the latch released and the door swung open. My office had its own challenges. The office chair would randomly turn. I would be typing and suddenly I'd be swinging around in my chair. I'd have to brace my feet against the desk to hold still so I could get my typing done. The house just wasn't right. Everyone who stayed there knew it whether or not they believed in those things and none ever returned to stay overnight twice. We're just not the type to cut and run simply because the house has quirks, though. The rent was great, the view rocked; so some minor quirks and feelings could just be gotten over. We weren't moving until we were good and ready.

I'm good and ready now.

I find the notion of moving incredibly motivating and head downstairs, stepping over and collecting another laundry pile on my way. I head down to the basement to find some boxes, shortening my hesitation time at the top of the stairs. *No time for fear indulgence.* I drop the laundry in the baskets and look around for the collapsed and stacked box pile. Creepy basement, haunted upstairs. This house just wasn't right from day one. We all knew it, but the view kept us blind to the urgency of getting out of there. I grab some boxes and run up the stairs, slamming the door shut once again, resting my back against it. *That's too many trips down there in one night for me.*

I head back up to her room to continue my search, taping up and dropping the boxes in a line along one wall. I mark one Goodwill, one Garbage, and a few Keep. I begin to sort her room using the boxes to organize as I go. I want to know everything she's been doing and plans to do. My tote begins to fill with new scraps of paper with more log-in information and phone numbers as I dig deeper into her room. *More to add to the list, more leads.* I find journal entries and spend a while just reading, sitting there amongst the boxes of her life. Her entries seem typical for a teen and I don't find anything that indicates any major upset beyond her legal trouble. *Legal trouble.* The words ring in my head and even in my exhausted state turn on a lightbulb of thought. *Probation, she's on probation.*

I drop what I'm doing and head back into my office to pull out her legal documents and find the agreement she signed in court. There's a total of sixteen legal case files in Sam's pile and it takes me a few minutes to locate the latest set. Thirteen are custody cases and three are legal trouble cases. I scan the requirements of probation and find that being in her court-approved home, ours, was a requirement. I was also to know where she was at all times, and I currently do not. *She's in violation of her probation.* The solution of how to hold her after capture starts to come together in my mind.

Sam's Legal Trouble:

*Sam had stolen some pills from her grandfather, who was losing his battle with cancer. She had given them to her friend Carla at her house, who then turned around and sold them at school. Everyone got caught, but Sam took the majority of the blame. While the other parents had gone into the school and proclaimed their children innocent in spite of video evidence, I had gone into it expecting Sam to accept responsibility and repair the harm done to everyone hurt by her actions. I never viewed the video. I didn't need to; I accepted the principal's word on it. This led to her being locked up in juvenile detention for three days and being handed a probation period of one year. She also lost her ability to take driver's education for one year. The worst part was the four-page letter from her grandfather telling her how low he thought of her. He didn't want anything to do with her. Samantha and I talked a long time about restorative justice and the need to repair the harm, to let the victims speak and be heard, and to repair it however you can. This man was the patriarch of the family, and he was losing his battle with a serious disease. Her theft went beyond the impact of a few pills. It had been a serious impact to every family member. Sammy accepted his anger, and eventually had a long sit down with him to repair the damage she had done. They repaired their relationship before he passed, which I'm grateful for to no end. I didn't want him to pass with this issue hanging between them.

Footnote to her legal trouble--Sam went on to successfully complete probation; becoming the probation officer's star client. He would often tell me that if every child in trouble accepted the harm they caused and worked to repair it as Sam did, there'd be far less recidivism among the teens and far less cynicism among adults toward teen delinquents. Sam did what she needed to, and it worked.

Another hour has passed and she still isn't home. My body is feeling the effects of too little sleep and too much coffee. Gary returns completely beaten down. He's ten years older than I am, and as hard as this is on me, it's harder on him. This is his grandchild that's out there, not just his daughter. When we took Sam in at the age of one, she became another one of our children, not just his biological grandchild. This is hitting on him on multiple levels, and I can do little for him but sit by his side while he cries in frustration. We talk a while about what we've learned and agree to tackle the phones together instead of him aimlessly driving around. We head upstairs to my office and get settled in for a long day of calls.

Gary gets up and goes to Sam's room to make his work calls. I lay my head on my keyboard, close my eyes, and listen to him making calls. I'm aware of his voice in the other room, lining the guys out on their daily tasks, and I yawn deeply. *Your child is missing and about to be sold.* The words act like an energy drink on my brain. I sit up, and I get to work locating our teen.

Gary comes back in and sits at my desk. He's cleared his schedule for the day and will take tomorrow off if needed. We use my notebook to make up a preliminary plan of attack.

"After we find her, I have an idea for what to do with her so she doesn't run again."

"What's that?" Gary asked.

"She's on probation--she signed a court agreement to remain here. I can call her in on a probation violation and get a warrant issued for her arrest."

"You're hard-core, Diane. You'd have our child picked up, hand-cuffed, put in a cop car, locked up?!" Gary looks at me like I might possibly be the most horrid mom alive.

"Yes, in a heartbeat. In lock-up I can get her wraparound services going, I can get her assessed by Jean, I can get her cleaned up and safe. So yes, I want to call her in on a violation. I wouldn't do this if it wasn't our best bet for immediate protection for her." I spend some time explaining my reasons and plans for services once she's secured. "Do you agree? I won't do this without you being on board."

"Yes." He agrees, but I'm unsure he means it.

"The cops will be called when they open up for the day, agreed?"

"Yes. It's time. She had hours to come home on her own."

"Just please don't let it be Officer Harris!" I laugh, but I'm dead serious. Any officer but him.

"Is he the one you've dealt with before at the school?"

"The one and only. The arrogant one who had us post a 'no parking' sign during the festival on the lot down below and then didn't enforce it so we looked like tools to all the angry people with no parking spaces."

"I remember him. He was a jerk."

"There's plenty of cops; I'm sure we'll get one of the other ones. Obviously Sam's going to need follow-up care; I'll start working that angle today and see what we can get for her."

"Can you also do the official Facebook post and get it out there?" *Gary hates Facebook, but he's about to see its positive power.*

"Absolutely. Let's also run through the name and number list with the cop and see if any names get a reaction from him. If any names are too familiar."

"Love it. And Jean. We need her to be in that jail immediately to do an assessment."

Any issues with Samantha, and Jean was our first call for mental health care. She had helped Samantha deal with and overcome both cases of juvenile PTSD she was given by her biological parents. I first hired Jean to counsel my children through my divorce from my first husband, and she'd been with us on our journey with Samantha from day one. She was already counseling Mathew and Katie when Samantha joined our family, so putting Sam with Jean was a natural addition to the client list. Jean was like a child's mind-guru. She knew how to make their little heads process all the crud that life throws at them.

"I'll call her today, fill her in, and have her standing by and ready for Sam's capture."

"Do you think she will?"

"Absolutely. She loves Sam. Any trouble with Sam and she's always cleared her schedule for me. I don't doubt she will again for something so serious."

"So post on Facebook, cops for warrant on a probation violation, track her down and capture her, get her in jail, assessed by Jean, and then... into rehab, most likely?"

"Sounds like a good start of a plan. Let's go with it and change as needed." Gary gives a small smile as if having a plan somehow makes this seem like we're in control and doing well with it.

Gary heads out to check the Winco and nearby town of LaCenter where she has some friends while I open Facebook to check for a response to my pleading message. No response. *How can you not respond, Boo? My heart is breaking--don't you care?*

I scan through Samantha's Facebook page looking for any clues as to her whereabouts. I'm a bit surprised to see her old flame Larry on her page. Years ago we had vacationed in Vegas and Samantha had promptly met a young boy by the name of Larry. He seemed like a nice kid and entertained Samantha all weekend in the arcade. He and his little sister and Samantha kept busy all weekend; as a trio, they went swimming together, played games, and ran the halls. He was Samantha's first vacation boyfriend. I knew he had remained her friend on Facebook, but wasn't aware he was still in the picture as more than just a distant acquaintance. Some of the comments he's left on her page makes him seem like a little more than a distant flame. I add Larry's name to my notebook, along with his Facebook name and url.

Sam's page is loaded with guy friends and comments from high school friends. I'm too tired to read anymore and take a moment to close my eyes and just think.

Have we done everything possible to this point?

HOUR 9:

Hello Again, Officer Harris

7:30-8:30 a.m.

If there's one cop I don't want to deal with on this, it's Officer Harris. He seems to be the only officer on duty whenever my child makes another bad choice and I just don't want to see him this morning. Any other officer but him. I don't know if it's his arrogance, or the fact it's always him I'm dealing with, or those orange sunglasses that remind me of a bug, but I close my eyes and say a little prayer that I get one of the other five cops the little town employs. Being a new believer, I'm confident my prayer will be answered.

I call the police station and ask to have an officer come out to take down the information on a runaway. Although some larger cities require a certain number of hours to pass before reporting it, our police department has so little to do they welcome reports. You can almost hear the joy in their voices as they get to fill out forms and dispatch officers. They're cute. Pretty much ineffective, but cute. The police department was like the fire department here; the fire truck drove through town every day. There were no fires to battle, but they would gear up and drive through town anyway. They'd wave to the kids, pull over and chat with the townsfolk, and drive back to the station where they'd wash the truck before backing it in its ready-to-go spot. The police served the same purpose in this tiny town. With five officers and a police chief, your odds of speeding through the two blocks of downtown area without getting pulled over were zero. They had nothing to do but park at the town's entrances and wait for anyone exceeding the 25mph limit. I'd see them slowly driving the two-block downtown area, or the small downtown neighborhoods, hour after hour with nothing to do, no one to pull over. A call about a runaway was sure to be met with multiple officers and I cringed at the thought the neighbors would see this. As long as none of the responding officers were that arrogant Officer Harris, I'd be fine.

Lesson Learned: Even if enough hours haven't passed to file an official report, at least make sure there's a recording of your voice or a report with a date and time stamp on it to start the countdown to when you can file a missing persons report. Know your local laws regarding reporting before you need the information.

There's a knock on the kitchen door and I go to answer it. I can see through the lace curtains well enough to recognize the orange wraparound sunglasses. I hold my hand on the doorknob and take in a deep breath. *Come on, I prayed.* I swing open the door and greet the officer on my porch, "Hello again, Officer Harris." Inside I swear I'm shriveling up. I think my stomach just vomited the gallons of coffee I've consumed into my body cavity. I hold the door open for him and he steps into the kitchen.

"Good morning. I understand young Miss Samantha has gone missing?" He slides his orange bug sunglasses to the top of his thinning hair and nails me with that familiar loser parent look he likes to give me. I have stared back at this man through some of my worst moments as a parent, and I wish just this once I wasn't having to do it again. His eyes bore right through mine and I feel our painful past together course throughout my body. I try to control the twisting of my mouth as the two years of interaction with this man flash through me, but I can't, so I turn to the sink.

Gary steps into the kitchen and extends his hand in greeting.

"Welcome--Officer Harris, was it?" Officer Harris exchanges greetings with Gary and follows him into the dining room. *It must be nice not to be the parent to always deal with these people. To have no history with any of them.* But that's why Gary works and I stay home--so I can deal with these people. *Like I did in October 2014....*

"We feel you should come to the school right away. The police are on their way." The school's receptionist sounded so concerned but I was positive there was a mistake. I'd run up there, get this cleared up, whatever it was, and be home in time to get ready for my job interview. *No problem. I got this.* It was going to be my time to go back to work and I'd worked hard to line up an interview with a company I really wanted to work for. I checked my watch; *plenty of time.* I raced up the hill to the high school, noting the police car out front. *Lovely.* I was obviously expected, as all eyes were on me when I walked into the office reception area. Voices became hushed as if a funeral was about to happen. The door to the principal's office opened and I was ushered in. Sitting at the table was Samantha, head down and fidgeting hands in her lap. Standing over her was Officer Harris.

"Hello ma'am; I'm Officer Harris and we have a bit of a problem here today." I didn't like the intimidating way he was standing over her so I walked over and placed myself between him and Sam. I knelt down so I was eye level with her.

"Sam, look at me please." Sam looked up. "Sam, why am I here right now? What are these people about to tell me? I'd like to hear it from you first."

Officer Harris cleared his throat behind me and began to speak. "Well, what we have here is a report of..."

I interrupted him without looking over my shoulder and continued with Sam. "Sam?"

Sam looked up at me and her eyes were huge green pools of tears. "Mom, I don't know what they're talking about. I didn't do what they're saying I did. I swear."

I patted her hand, told her we'd get it handled, and went to take the other chair at the table. Officer Harris stood off to the side and nailed me with the coldest look I think I've ever received. "As I was saying, what we have here is a report of marijuana brownies being distributed on school grounds."

I stared back at Officer Harris and then looked to the principal. "Is this true? Has a report been made? By whom? Where are these brownies?"

The principal confirmed the report and I looked at Sam. "Sam? Anything to add?"

Sam looked at me and again claimed she had no idea what they were talking about. "Mom, they're just brownies. I got them from Mommy's."

I looked at Officer Harris and the principal and explained that in our lives I'm Mom, the day-to-day Mom, and her biological Mom is called Mommy. Her biological Mom holds a medical-use card because of her health conditions, and grows a few plants in their home. We are aware of this but not worried as the use is not around Samantha.

"I think first we need to know whether or not there's pot in the brownies, yes? If not, I'm here on a report of brownies being shared, and that's not a crime."

Officer Harris pulled out a large peanut jar with a few crumbles of dried-out- looking brown stuff on the bottom. "That's the brownies? Are those even brownies?"

"Yes ma'am, they are." Officer Harris poured out a small piece of brownie on the table to show me. "I smelled it, and it smells of mari-juana." The principal told me that two students claimed Sam shared them and they got high off them. I asked Officer Harris if the brownies had been tested.

"No ma'am; I'll send them off to the state lab for testing."

"Can't you field test them so I know if there's been a crime committed?"

He told me he had a field test kit, but that's he's never tried out the new one issued. He went to his squad car to retrieve it, came back and tested the brownies. He had to read the instructions twice and seemed very unsure of what he was doing. The brownies tested positive for marijuana. I turned to Sam.

"Anything to say yet? They tested positive, Sam. You've just been busted with pot brownies at school."

Sam started sobbing. "Mom, I swear I didn't know. I swear I didn't. Mommy gave me the brownies and said I could have them."

I looked at Officer Harris. "What now? Is she being arrested?" Samantha started hysterically sobbing and I sat next to her and held her hand.

"No, I'm not arresting her; charges will be filed, though, and we'll be in touch. You can take her home."

The principal let me know she was suspended until further notice, handed me my white envelope of suspension papers, and told Sam to collect her items from her locker. I checked the wall clock and saw my interview just started without me. I wanted to cry, but one look at my daughter and I realized this just wasn't my time. Not yet.

It had taken some phone calls, but once we had proven to the District Attorney that Samantha was the victim of an unfortunate mix-up of brownie containers, and raised the concerns about the testing that had been done on site, they had dropped the charges. Officer Harris had made it his personal mission to drop by the house to check on "young Miss Samantha" regularly after that. Each time he would stand there with his hands on his hips, orange bug sunglasses on his head, and look at me with obvious disdain. I would report that all was well and stare back with equal disdain. We didn't like each other; that much was clear.

I brace myself for yet another round with this officer and give him the run-down on what happened the night before and what we've learned since then. Another officer arrives and I shrink in embarrassment as I see the neighbors beginning to take notice of the two squad cars out front. They're standing out front of their homes pointing at our house, and I wish the ground would just swallow me up. I close the door behind officer number two and sit down at the dining room table with Gary and Officer Harris.

I go very quiet as I watch the scene in front of me. You know those movies where a child goes missing and suddenly their living room is full of police and activity? It really does happen that way, and it's surreal when it's happening. These people sit there discussing our daughter. *These people are here because SAM IS MISSING.* The words cause a body ache so severe I feel I might lose my mind right there on the spot. I fight back the tears and pain and focus on their instructions.

It was going to be a long haul--that was their message. Settle in, they don't get found if they don't want to. Assemble your lists, make your calls, post your search. We'll keep our eyes open, but don't expect her back until she's ready; kids can stay underground for months. They sound like a brochure. Like they're hiding behind their statistics and usual results. Reports in hand, the second cop leaves. Officer Harris turns to me.

"You know with her being on probation you can call this in as a violation."

"Yes, we thought about that. I'll be calling her PO this morning and getting that going. Will it be this town that issues the warrant?"

"No, it will come out of Vancouver. That's where her legal case is." He gives me more information on contacting her probation officer and what to say to her PO that will move it along quicker. I realize that it's only because he's so familiar with our family that he knows to give me this information. *You did answer my prayer, Lord--just not how I thought it should be answered.*

Officer Harris slides his orange wraparound sunglasses back over his eyes. He looks like an orange bug and it's hard not to smile at the sight of him. I'm happy to close the door as he walks back to his patrol car, and yet I have a newfound appreciation for him.

I look at Gary. "Well--by now we're the talk of the town, you know."

"I'm sure of it. Did you see that old lady that rides her bike every day? She came to a complete stop and just watched our house while the police cars were here."

We both sigh. We left Vancouver because Samantha had destroyed our reputations in the neighborhood. Our home had gone underwater during the recession and we took the chance to dump the home, dump the shame she had brought us, and move to this town to lick our wounds, give her a fresh start, and recover financially. With such low rent, it wouldn't be a problem if we stayed put for two years. But of course Samantha had ripped us apart in the new town as well. Maybe one more move....

"Okay, police report filed. It's time to do the Facebook official post and generate some leads."

"What about the map? Do you want to head down there yet?"

"Not quite. I really want to get her Facebook post done, and then we'll see if we have time to go hunt down these addresses. I'm not sure what kind of response we'll get, but I'm betting it gets shared a few times. I know you hate Facebook, but it's our best bet for getting the word out."

"I'm fine with whatever you need to do online for this. I'll handle the ground, driving to wherever you get a lead for."

"We got this. We're smarter than these creeps."

"I'll still kill them if I find them."

"Oh, I know--but first we get her to safety."

Gary and I head upstairs and he sees the row of boxes.

"Why the boxes?"

"Because when we find her, we're moving. We all hate the trains, this house just isn't right, and now our child has jumped to get away from...us? The trains? This house? This town? That school? I don't know yet, but I know she needs a change of environment. We all do."

"I think it's too soon. She's only been gone the night. I don't want her coming back and feeling like she doesn't have a home anymore."

"I respect that, but Gary...even if she comes home now, she's not going to be up in this room anymore. Even if she comes in the door this very minute, our time here has to end."

As if to drive my point home, a coal train goes by, the heavy loud carts screeching along the tracks. That vacant block isn't enough space to keep the sounds from driving into your skull every five to ten minutes as another one goes by. With an average of 125 carts to pass per train, the screeching drags out for a few minutes, during which no meaningful conversation can be held. Gary tries twice but has to keep stopping when I can't hear him. By the time the last train cart goes by, and the ringing intersection guards raise back into position, Gary is on board with moving, nodding his head.

"Okay, but what if she comes back today? You have her room in boxes."

"I do. I'll explain she opted out and that we're moving like she wanted to. That she's bunking with me until then. I'll make it fun, Gary--I won't traumatize her with it. Admit it, though; you're excited at the thought of getting out of here."

For the first time in hours Gary smiles.

"Yeah, it's time. Let's get our kid back and get the hell out of this place."

We smile at each other in spite of our child being out there; we smile because we know it's the right thing to do.

HOUR 10:

Click Post

8:30-9:30 a.m.

Gary goes downstairs to make some business calls, so I tackle finding a good shot of her for a missing poster. I put my fingers on the keyboard, but I can't seem to figure out what to do. I close my eyes for just a second to rest them and refocus. I wake up a few minutes later, fingers still on keyboard, neck stiff from hanging forward. I stand up and jump up and down a few times to come alive.

I pour another cup of coffee, sit down at the table, and search through my iPad's picture file for a good shot of Sam to use for a poster. It's a strange thing choosing a picture for a missing poster. You want a recent shot, but one that shows them in a natural state so people will recognize them. They won't recognize your child if you use a prom picture, as your child is likely not walking around in a ball gown. I choose one of her at the farm in her Beatles t-shirt. She looks so happy in this picture. She was just learning to drive and was walking up to me to ask for the keys so she could drive down the driveway. The farm has a ¼-mile driveway and it's been the teaching grounds for my three kids to learn to drive. It's private, so none of them needed a driver's permit to start with the basics of going up and down the long driveway. She has a smirk in the picture, her hair is blowing in the breeze, the sunshine is on her, and she looks happy.

The tears start again as I revisit this happy memory from just last month, captured only in pixels on a plastic screen. What if this is all I'll ever get? I clutch the iPad picture to my chest and quietly indulge the tears for a moment. *The crying has to stop. It's interfering. Stop it.* Putting down the iPad I go to the kitchen, splash cold water on my face, and hold the dishcloth against my eyes. I don't move the cloth but just hold it there, pressing it into my skin, my hands clutched in fists. The tears threaten to start again and I struggle not to lose control. *SHE'S BEING TRIED OUT AND SOLD, MOM. TWO MEN ARE CRAWLING OVER HER RIGHT NOW.* The words scream through my head and my last hold of not losing it slips away. I scream at the top of my lungs into the towel. I scream over and over until I can't scream anymore. *My baby. My poor baby.* I sit down on the floor with my back to the kitchen cabinet, curl up in the corner by the wall, lower my head, and allow my heart to finish breaking. I sob into the dish towel for a few long minutes. I sob until there's no more tears. I allow my breathing to slow, my thoughts to clear, and my chest to loosen its death grip on my heart.

Taking a deep breath I stand up, wash my face, and get back to the task at hand: locating my child and reclaiming her from manipulating pigs. I promise myself someday I'll sit and take the time to grieve over all of this. Just not today.

I sit down with my coffee and open the app Skitch to upload her photo. I add in her vital information and last place seen. The color of the text looks terrible next to her shirt color and I start trying out different ones. *Your child is missing and you're playing with font color. You're creating a missing child poster.* The thought seems so strange to me. *Other people do this, not me.*

You're now one of them.

You're the mother of a runaway.

That thought sends a cold chill through my body.

I finish the poster and save it as a new picture. It looks bizarre there on the screen next to the original. One is a happy child, one is a runaway poster. I remember posting this particular shot of Sam after coming home from the farm. It was a positive thing. Now it's a runaway poster.

I sit down to make the official Facebook post about our missing child. I pull up the photo from Skitch with her info, load it on Facebook, and request anyone with information to please contact me. I hesitate to hit post; somehow that makes all of this official. *It is official, and time's ticking.* I hit post and take a deep breath.

Friends and family are up and the news is beginning to spread. My phone starts to ring as friend after friend calls to offer support and see what they can do. I keep the calls short, but need to make sure no one has information on Sam that I need. None do.

Lesson Learned: Purchasing an inexpensive phone specifically for the search is a good idea. It keeps your main line open and eliminates answering calls that have nothing to do with locating your child.

Dear Lord, I know I just discovered you yesterday, but I need you. The tears start to flow down my cheeks as I sit in silent prayer with my head back and face to heaven. *I don't know what to do. My baby is gone and I'm scared. I don't know what to do, I don't know how to fix this. I'm not Christian-y enough yet to know how to do this. Help us. Please help us. Amen.* I take a moment and just let His peace calm me down. *Think.* It's a common voice in my head when faced with challenges. I think my way out of them. *Think.*

8:49 a.m. Facebook message received from girlfriend Virginia

"I'm saying prayers for you and your family." These messages bring me more comfort than the senders realize.

I assemble our list of numbers and prioritize them. Check in with the police, call her probation officer Roy, call every friend we have a number for, check with her biological parents and notify them, grandparents, and other family members who might know something, and start going through the list of national organizations.

Gary comes back upstairs and we head upstairs to the office to make our calls.

"You've never sat with me while I do Sam calls."

"I know. Fifteen years and all those cases and I've never actually seen how you pull off what you do."

In the fifteen years we had been raising Samantha, I had prepared the papers for sixteen different court battles. Each set required hours of calls, emails, texts, faxes, and meetings, followed by massive information to assemble. Gary had never been home to see any of it until the final papers were ready to be signed and taken to court. Her biological father had been a challenge for us since he had shown up on the scene when she was two years old. A DNA test proved him correct in his claims, leading to a very uncomfortable phone call between myself and the man and his mom, who thought they were Sam's father and grandmother. Not once had Gary had the time to see what it took to keep this child safe legally. This would be his first look at child advocacy in the real feet-on-the-ground sense.

I start with another plea to Samantha on the only site I'm almost guaranteed she'll visit: Facebook.

9:22 a.m. I post to Facebook:

"Boo, please come home. Please. My heart is breaking. I know you can read this. Please stop doing these things and let us help you. Your dad's been driving all night looking for you. Please, Sam..."

9:27 a.m. Facebook message response to Paul

"Sam's Facebook alert is done and has 99 shares already!"

I check my Facebook and see friend requests coming in. Some are from Sam's friends. I check their pages and see they've shared my missing child post on their pages. They're beginning to buzz about Sam running away. I post a heartfelt plea for information, knowing they'll see it.

The phone rings again and I close the iPad to focus on the phone calls. If I'd had someone to help with the Facebook page, I might have seen the messages coming in to the "other" folder from Samantha's schoolmates, filling me in on what they knew of her activities over the past few months and their concerns. Because I had to split my time between Facebook and the phone calls, that information came to me hours later.

Lesson Learned: Having an extra pair of hands to manage the social media page is beyond necessary. Someone needs to babysit that account, watch for new requests, messages in both the inbox and "other" folder, and comment posts. List all leads and follow up on them. Teens do not want their friends to be on the streets, and a heartfelt plea can work wonders to break through their tough exteriors and get them talking. This is not the time to lecture them; this is the time to be quiet, take notes, and keep them talking.

HOUR 11:
Call Central

9:30-10:30 a.m.

9:34am Facebook message received from girlfriend Virginia
"I've placed you all on my church's prayer chain." Being placed on
a prayer chain and knowing complete strangers were praying for us
touched my heart deeply. As we made calls, perfect strangers were car-
rying on the fight for Samantha through prayer.

We sit side-by-side at my desk and divide up the call list. He takes
his list and says he wants to watch me do one first. Each call is basically
the same...

"Hello. I'm Diane and my daughter Samantha jumped from her
second-story window last night at midnight. We don't know where she
is, but we've learned she may be in the company of a known pimp and
sex trafficker. Can you help us?" I make it through my intro before the
tears start trying to slip out again. It makes seeing my notes even harder, and it becomes a constant struggle to not feel the pain so I won't
cry. After a few calls I find it easier to get through the information-
gathering without falling apart.

Gary heads to Sam's room with his list. I listen as he makes his first
call. "Hello, I'm Gary Geister and last night my daughter Samantha

jumped from her second-story window..." My heart breaks for this man, but I don't have time to help him deal with it right now. *Later*. As soon as I hang up on one call, another comes in. The national organizations have their local branches calling, along with family and friends. I pull out a notebook and start listing numbers and information for each call to keep them straight.

We've become a call center, with barely enough break between calls to update each other. Gary and I spend another hour making calls. We catch sight of each other on our calls through the open doorways and share a look of exhaustion and pain. I hold up my notes for him to see, and he holds up his for me to see. When our calls end I call out to him, "Any luck?" He just hangs his head and shakes it back and forth. He gives a deep sigh as both phones start ringing again.

I finally reach Roy, the probation officer.

"Diane, I got your message--what happened?" Roy is obviously confused, as Samantha had been doing so well and meeting all the requirements. He is as blindsided as we were.

"Roy I'm just figuring out what's been going on for the past few months, but it's looking like she was sucked into sex trafficking. From what we understand last night she was 'tried out' and possibly sold to two men. Roy, I'm desperate--what do I do?"

Roy explains to me that beyond locating her, getting her locked up on a probation violation would be the best bet for holding her. "But you know that will only work for a few days; beyond that, she can take off again."

"And then what? And endless cycle of running away, probation violations and lock-up, only to release and start over again?"

"Sadly, yes. There isn't much more that can be done, legally. We'll hold her longer and longer though, each time." His words offer me zero comfort.

He explains the process of getting the warrant issued, finding her, locking her up, and the follow-up court appointment where I can request additional lock-up time. "But understand, Diane, this is a first-time violation; extra time would be unheard-of."

"Unheard-of but possible is all I need, Roy. You get the warrant going and we'll find her."

"Bring her straight to juvenile detention when you locate her, and I'll have the warrant waiting there for you. They can take her straight into custody. But remember, they can't hold her long."

I hang up and breathe a sigh of relief. We have someplace to take her that's secure, where they can't reach her. If she was sold, there would people who would be out money when Sam was removed from the street. I didn't doubt someone would come looking for payback. Getting Sam somewhere secured where these people couldn't touch her was our only goal. I wait for Gary to finish his call and give him the news. It feels like the first bit of progress, knowing what to do with her when we find her. We discuss what to do with her after the three days in juvenile detention are up.

"I'll argue for additional time while we figure it out. If I can get us an extra day or two, it gives me an extra day or two to find her follow-up care."

Gary tells me about his calls with the National Human Trafficking Resource Center as well as The National Center for Missing and Exploited Children. Both places had some good resources and information, but neither could help with the immediate issue: locating Sam before she was sold. "Diane, The Center for Missing and Exploited Children told me 800,000 children are reported missing every year. 800,000!" (NCMEC) He explains that The Human Trafficking Resource Center has a hotline for calling in tips and missing children (NHTRC). "Thoughts? Do I call her in?" We agree and I add them to my list to call later.

I share with him my findings on the Polly Klaas Foundation website, www.pollyklaas.org (Polly Klaas). "Gary, they offer a really great service in helping you locate your child, but the review of your information alone can take 24 hours, I don't think we can spare that kind of time. What do you think?"

"Let's submit it and get it going, and then we can always cancel it if--I should say when--we find her."

I agree and spend a few minutes filling out their form. Last seen wearing... contact information...the basics. *I hate this.* We get it done and hit submit. *Let the 24 hours to review begin.*

I tell him about my earlier call with Shared Hope International. "Gary, it's so sad. There are 100,000 children bought, sold and rented in the US every year. (Shared Hope)." I take him to their website, www.sharedhope.org and show him some of the information they offer. "Look Gary, I think is how they got to Sam. From what I'm learning in her room and from her friends, it sounds like this is how this guy Higgs got to her, right in our local park."

Many pimps often use a "lover-boy" technique to recruit girls from middle and high schools. A lover-boy will present himself as a boyfriend and woo the girl with gifts, promises of fulfilled dreams, protection, adventure – whatever she perceives she is lacking. Traffickers use social media sites to recruit teenagers. After securing her love and loyalty, he will force her into prostitution (Shared Hope).

"Gary, Sam can't be a statistic."

"She won't be. She has us, and we're not letting this happen to her." He stands up and pushes his chair back forcefully. "No, I'm not standing for this. We didn't raise this child for all these years, fight all these cases just to let some perverted pigs claim her. Not happening on our watch." His head is actually turning red in anger as he stares down at the website page that exposes more truth to us about what's happening right now to our girl. The stories are hard to read; the truth that it could be our daughter is harder to accept.

10:00 a.m. Facebook message received from an old classmate of mine from childhood

"Can you phone track her?" Unfortunately, Samantha had lost her phone privileges a month ago and didn't have a phone. Or so I thought at the time. The mystery phone charger has yet to be fully explained.

Gary goes back to Sam's room to make calls to his family. During one call I hear his voice rising and becoming more tense and angry. I finish my call and wait for him to finish his. He comes in with information. Sam's biological father has been sneaking into town and picking her up and taking her to Oregon. He's been providing her a room and allowing her to have sex there. He also buys her cigarettes, pot, and alcohol.

"Who told you this?!"

"Believe it or not, the idiot himself."

"What?! Why would he own up to something like contributing to the delinquency of a minor?!"

"Because it's him, Diane--he's an idiot. It's one of the reasons we have her and not him. He doesn't have a dad bone in his body. He's just trash."

"So he's been transporting her across state lines, contributing to the delinquency... anything else, or can I go stomp his face in?" I'm fuming. I can't remember being this angry. *Yes, you can. The night he brought her home at age eight with that humongous purple and black eye, and a million stories to go with it.*

I sit there feeling my blood boiling; I'm enraged. His rights to visits were terminated when she came home with the black eye, and terminated completely when we adopted her, at his request. He was facing more jail time for unpaid child support and offered to relinquish his rights so we could adopt her if I'd make the bill go away. I did, but with the agreement he would disappear until she turned eighteen, at which time they could spend every day together if that's what they wanted. But until that age, I was done dealing with legal cases, bruises, drama, and him. He had agreed fully and we adopted Samantha on Valentine's Day 2014. To hear he had come sneaking around behind our backs, transporting our child across state lines, and giving her a room to party in was more than I wanted to hear.

"He feels bad. He told her she could come stay with him and his girlfriend. That if she couldn't stand living with us, his door was always open."

I have to slowly close my eyes and take his words in, because they might just be the thing that pushes me over the limit of what I can handle. I exhale the air like daggers and feel my heart squeezing with anger and hatred. "He told her she could come stay with him?! You have to be joking! Has he seen or heard from her since last night?"

"No, but he'll call if he does. I didn't want to sound angry with him; we may need him for information later."

"I understand that, Gary, but you understand me on this point very clearly. I despise that man. I despise everything he is and everything he stands for. I've spent how many hours over how many years fighting him in court every time he had a new crap job and felt he could raise Sam himself? I finally, finally get him gone and you're telling me he's been offering her a place to stay? Why? What did she tell him about living here? How did she justify it...what, three rooms and everything she wants wasn't good enough? This is really out of line, even for him!"

"Just let me handle him. Don't even worry about him right now, Diane. You do your calls and I'll handle this guy, okay?"

I agree--not because I don't want to rip her bio dad limb from limb, but because the negative energy he creates in me is taking my focus off finding Sam. I take a few deep breaths, and I let it and him go...for now.

Lesson Learned: If someone needs to be dealt with that one of the search parties doesn't get along with, have someone else ask the questions and handle interactions with that person. This isn't the time to have petty arguments about old issues. This is information-gathering time only. If you need to approach someone you have a negative history with, hand off the duty so the mission goal is still accomplished.

The phone ringing interrupts the discussion and Gary's off to answer it. From the sound of the call, it's work-related. *I can't imagine trying to run a job while going through all of this. He thinks he's coming back into her life and offering her a place to stay?!* I feel my head swimming in the anger like a whirlpool. Years of legal work, years of counseling, and he thinks he can just waltz back in and play Dad?! *Maybe he'd like to receive his $25,000 back child support bill? I wish I was a mob daughter right now--I'd just make him disappear.* I stare out the window and envision the many ways I'd like to hurt this man, while I twist a letter opener round and round in the palm of my hand. I look at my watch and realize I just wasted five minutes staring into space, have given myself deep purple welts across my palms, and all while envisioning the slow torturous death of her biological father. *Well--that's not showing much brotherly love, Diane.* I wonder briefly if believing means you have to love and accept EVERYONE. Maybe there was a loophole somewhere for truly vile people. I'd have to ask D.W. about that during our next Bible study. Sometimes the depth of my anger toward people who hurt my children scares me. Ultimately though, focusing on bio-Dad isn't helping the problem.

10:17 a.m. Email from Sue

"Checked again, still no Sam at Winco."

Gary pokes his head in the office. "Why don't you sleep for a bit, and I'm going to go drive around the old neighborhood and see if she's there with her friends." As much as I'd like to argue, my swimming head is demanding a little down time.

Gary tucks me in and I hear him drive off. I lay there and wait for sleep to come. I check the clock--10:22 a.m. *It's been a little over 10 1/2 hours and still no Sam. Child, where are you?! I need to check Facebook. I should be calling those numbers from her room and find out if she's there.* My brain refuses to shut off. I turn over and hope that a repositioning of my legs will bring about sleep. My legs hurt from being awake so long, and yet feel like I need to stretch them. I lie there and stretch my legs out as far as they'll go, then pull them in and turn over. Adjust the pillows. Legs hurting again. I roll over and stretch them out again. *Oh, this is ridiculous--just get up. No, I need sleep. Then shut up so I can sleep. Is Sam sleeping? How can I sleep when my child is missing? How does Paul sleep after months of this? Is this our new normal?* My thoughts won't shut down long enough to sleep and I feel cold all over. I begin to cry as I say a prayer. *Lord, I'm not very good at this yet. But I'm scared, I'm exhausted, and I need to sleep. I'm not sure if this is how this all works, but can I just lay my head on your lap and let your peace be enough to let me sleep a while? Can you just come sit in bed with me and let me rest on you a minute? Please?* I instantly feel a flooding warmth and peace flow through me. Sitting there in my bed, leaned up against my headboard, I felt He held me and stilled my thoughts, and I fell into the most restful minutes of sleep I can remember.

HOUR 12:
New Friends And Info

10:30-11:30 a.m.

I'm wide awake and it's been only a few minutes of sleep. I feel re-
freshed, though, at least enough to keep going. I head to the kitchen
and peek outside. The Jeep is still gone. *Maybe he got lucky and found
her.* I check my phone, but no messages. I message Sam a few more
times on Facebook to see if she'll respond. No reply. No calls from
Gary. I dial his number to check on his search.

"Any sign of her?"

"You slept less than an hour. Go back to bed."

"I can't sleep--I will later. I promise. No sign of her?"

"No. Now go sleep. I'll bring you home some food--but first sleep."

I agree with no intention of sleeping; it's just easier than arguing
about it.

It's strange, but when I look outside it's a beautiful sunny spring
morning, and yet inside this house the world is cold and dark. I watch a
woman drive past the house and I'm struck by the normalcy of her life
right now versus the complete chaos and pain going on in here. *Is this
life now, walking around in a fog? How do the parents with kids missing
for months or years learn to handle this?*

I check my Facebook and see a message from Sam's friend Mary as well as three others. They all want to know if Sam is okay. I reply to each that we're desperate to get her back, that we hear she's with a pimp and sex trafficker, and do they have any info whatsoever that could help us save Sam. I place no blame, accuse none of them, and play up the distraught mom routine to appeal to whatever hearts they have. Some, I suspect, are in on it, but I maintain my composure so I don't drive anyone away.

In the "other" folder I find messages from more of Samantha's classmates.

10:40 a.m. Facebook "other" message received from classmate of Sam's--

"Hello Diane, I am a student that attends Ridgefield high school. I previously attended with your daughter, Sammy. I saw your post about how she went missing and I wanted to inform you that I do have some information about her but very little. I saw the post and quickly messaged her to ask her some questions. If you have time I'd love to talk! I do ask that I stay anonymous please, as I do not wish for no one to know. Thank you for your time and hope to hear from you soon."

This became typical of almost every single teen I talked with. None wanted it to be known they had talked to a parent, yet they all wanted me to have the information.

10:41 a.m. Facebook "other" message received from classmate of Sam's--

"I'm sorry to hear Sammy ran away. She's been partying every weekend for months. I tried to warn her she was being dangerous, but she didn't care. She said she wouldn't ever stop, that she couldn't."

I respond with a question--"Did she say she couldn't, or wouldn't stop?"

The response--"Couldn't."

This tells me Sam may not be able to stop, because my daughter rarely says the words "can't" or "couldn't." *If she **can't** stop, there's a reason.*

**10:50 a.m. Facebook "other" message received
from Samantha's classmate-**

"Hi. Sorry to hear about Sam. I see her get in strange cars after school and leave. I asked her who the people were and she said family. Just thought you should know in case it helps."

It does, as Samantha has no family in the area that would be picking her up at school. I respond, "Do you remember a car make or model, or what they looked like or where they went?"

They respond, "No but she says she stays with her bio dad on some weekends, and I know she got some stuff from Mall 205 a few times."

The phones don't stop ringing as concerned friend after concerned friend calls to offer us prayers and well wishes, and another hour passes without a break in between calls.

I pull out the information for our insurance and call customer service to find out about after-care options. The news is disheartening. They have a long process to go through and then I'll still have to get approval from the one guy in charge of these things for two states. After a number of transfers, I finally reach a sympathetic ear.

"Ma'am, you'll need to get approval for offsite rehabilitation. I can give you a messaging service number for that department."

"Do they have a fax number or direct number so I can send them any information they might need to make their decision?"

"No ma'am; just leave a message and they'll get back to you as soon as they can."

With a limited three-day lock-up when we find her, the words "as soon as they can" simply aren't cutting it for me. "Can you tell me please the name of the decision-maker?"

"Oh, that's Mr. Bruce--all final decisions after completing the process wind up on his desk."

I thank the lady and hang up. I call the central messaging service. "Hello ma'am, I was just talking to a Mr. Bruce somewhere in your department and we got disconnected. Do you have a call back number?" *Lord, forgive me for lying.* She puts me on hold for a second and comes back with a new number for central messaging in his department. I thank her, hang up, and call the number to leave a message asking someone to call me, that's it's very urgent. Not content to wait, I call another number for customer service and explain that I needed to fax a paper to Mr. Bruce that was requested, but that I didn't catch the fax number. *Lord, can I run a tab for lying today?* The lady puts me on hold, and comes back with a fax number. I thank her and promptly fax a request for immediate contact to Mr. Bruce. Running the phone number and fax number through reverse search, I come up with one more number that seems tied to this approval department. I dial the number and am surprised to find the voicemail of the big decision-maker himself. With no time to prepare for what feels like the audition of my life, I wait for the beep which is coming up way too fast. Beep.

"Hello, sir. I'm Diane and my daughter Samantha jumped from her second-story window last night and ran away. She is believed to be in the company of a pimp and sex traffickers. I am trying to get approval for her to receive after care at a secured lock-up facility. If she isn't locked up, she will run, or they'll come for her. They were supposed to be selling her last night to two men who were trying her out." I allow the natural catch in my voice to come out, and let this person on the other end hear my barely contained tears and pain. I need him to see us as more than just everyone else. I need him to care like never before. "We will have her assessed while we have her locked up on a probation violation, but we need approval to be ready to go for after care. We have a deadline we're working under. They won't hold her for more than a few days. I NEED to have her after care lined up, approved and ready to go. No gaps in secured hold. Please help us, please approve her file." I leave my contact information clearly, repeat my name, and hang up. I wonder if that will help or get me in trouble for calling him directly.

My phone rings almost immediately, it's Mr. Bruce. *Again with no preparation time, dang it.* I answer the phone. "Hello."

"Hello Diane, I received your voicemail. The first thing I have to ask is how you got this number? No one has this number!" He's laughing a little and I'm relieved.

"I reverse searched your other numbers through a program I have.

Sorry. I just really need approval to be set. I'm working against traffickers trying to sell my child." I explain our time constraints and that if they let her go from juvenile, she'll be back on the streets immediately. "After care is a must, Mr. Bruce. She must have somewhere secure to go while we get her cleaned up and figure out what led to this."

"I understand, but our policy is to do the evaluation in-house, and then do counseling in her local medical center. If those options don't work, then we move into the next phase of inpatient care. There's an entire process."

"Mr. Bruce, I understand you have policies and regulations to work under. I do. But this is that one time in your career where the extraordinary is needed. This is the one time where you need to step outside of those bounds and make a decision based on what's right. And what's right is to not put my child at risk on the streets while boxes get checked. I'll bring in her childhood private-paid counselor so it doesn't cost you a penny, and have the assessment done right there in juvenile detention. Her counselor has been with her since childhood, she's court-ready with her reports, and she's highly respected in this community. We have no problem paying her to do the assessment and faxing it to you. Could you approve her then? Could it be set up before she gets released? I don't know what else to do here, sir--I'm begging you to make the most meaningful decision of your career on Sammy's behalf. Please!" I'm almost in tears as I beg for Sam's approval.

Mr. Bruce goes quiet. *Please Lord, open his heart. Please. Let him hear my need.* "Diane, I like you. You're a mom I can respect. I like that you fight so hard for your daughter, even to the point of tracking down my personal desk number. No one has it by the way, so no sharing it! I only give out the central service number or the fax number, never both. I'll tell you what, you find her and I'll see to it that she has the approval you need. I'll go out on a limb for you and Samantha and trust."

"Thank you! What do I need to do from here?" The relief is tremendous.

"I have a facility in mind that I want you to check out. It's NW Behavioral. It's in Oregon and a bit of a drive for you, but it's a secured facility, and a good one."

I take down the name and website and ask him about financing and insurance.

"I have a couple in mind that if you like, I'll approve you for full coverage past $5000."

The amount gags me, but I know from preliminary web checks on after care, the facilities charge hundreds per day and Sam would need long-term care. I saw some places that wanted $10,000 down and hundreds a month in fees and charges. $5,000 total is a good deal. I quickly accept it.

"Go get her, Mom; we'll talk soon."

I hang up and sit in stunned silence. Huge relief tears roll out and down my cheeks. *All we have to do is find you, Sam. We're coming, sweetheart; we're coming and we're not letting them have you. Thank you, Lord Jesus, for opening his heart to see our need. Thank you for making him hear and respond.*

My Facebook messaging notifications are lighting up as Sam's friends share with me her activities over the past few months that have concerned them. I'm taking screen shots of every conversation so I can remember who told me what. I shoot back quick questions to those I feel might have more information. Some seem like they just want in on the action, and them I leave in the "other" folder. If they seem to really know Sam or have information, I immediately send them a friend request. This opens up their Facebook pages to me so I can see everything posted if their security settings were blocking content to people not on their friends list. As each one accepts me I scan through their old posts to see anything that Samantha has liked or commented on. I look through their pictures to see if I can see Sam in any of them, and save copies of every photo I find with Samantha in it. Their messages tell me Sam has been going to parties at night, sneaking out after I go to bed. She has a whole separate night life that ends with her climbing back into her room right before her dad gets up. The pictures I've saved from their social media pages back up their claims.

She has a double life. All those excuses for being tired for homeschool... I'm cramping, Mom; I don't feel well, Mom; I didn't sleep well,

Mom...and I bought every excuse. The reality was she was out partying at night and living on a couple hours of sleep per night. *Explains the grades, too. I wonder if she had a choice, though.* My emotions swing between anger and fear, and the combination is mentally and physically draining. *How could she do this?! I want her home. Is she okay? My poor baby! How could she not tell us?! What have they done to her? I just want her back. I just want her safe. Oh, Sam.....*

The mental back and forth is as distracting as the tears, which thankfully have begun to dry up. I don't stop hurting; I just can't make any more. Until I stop looking for her and I go still. When I am still, that's when I hear the little girl laughing, her voice ringing through the halls. I can't bear the silence, the stillness. I run from it by searching harder, making more calls, drinking more coffee. Anything but sit still and hear her little voice, "Mom, I love you so so much" followed by a peck on the tip of my nose. Too late, the stillness gets to me and the tears begin again. *I want my little girl back, I want my girl back. She's not theirs, she's mine.* I cry out for a while to no one but the now-still voices in the hall. *I want my girl back...*

HOUR 13:
Driving In Circles

11:30 a.m.-12:30 p.m.

Another hour has ticked by. It's been twelve hours now. *Has she eaten? Did she sleep? Is she still alive...?*

Gary gets home and walks in with a bag of McDonald's burgers. The food looks as appealing as I feel. We leave it in the bag on the counter, untouched.

The phone rings. I'm halfway through the call with yet another organization when another call comes in. The overlapping calls continue. "Hello. I'm Diane and my daughter Samantha jumped from her second-story window last night at midnight. We don't know where she is, but we've learned she may be in the company of a known pimp and sex trafficker. Can you help us?"

I'm beginning to sound like a broken record. My throat is raw from saying the words over and over again, but I push on. Maybe the next call can offer real help. Maybe the next call will have hope to offer. Call after call ends in frustrated helplessness. Once she's found, they're lined up to help us with counseling and rehab, if approved by Mr. Bruce, but nothing can be done until she's located. Gary and I take a break downstairs and leave our phones upstairs. We spend ten minutes in silence just thinking, and exchanging a lot of deep sighs.

"Ready to get back to it?"

Gary shakes his head slowly. "No, I'm not. I feel like I should be out looking again."

"Where would you even begin, Gary? She could be anywhere right now. The odds of you driving past her are so low it makes no sense. Stay, do the calls with me, and go out when we have a target."

"I know, but this is so frustrating. I feel like we're just spinning our wheels while she's out there, God knows where, having what done to her? What, Diane? What?!" he practically screams the last what. *He's cracking.* "I can't take this; I can't." He leans over, puts his fists to his face and just sobs his heart out. I sit in stunned silence, staring at the floor, my heart breaking for him.

"I know, Gary. I know. But we have to get back to the phones. We have to keep trying. Someone could have a lead."

I get up and go rub his shoulders while he gathers himself.

"I'm okay. I'm sorry. I shouldn't lose it like that." He wipes his eyes and struggles to regain control. "It's just making me sick knowing what's been done to her. I can't get my head around it. I can't." He looks at me with such raw pain on his face. *I'd give anything for him not to be going through this.*

"It's okay, Gary, we are both having our moments. We just can't both lose it at the same time--agreed?" We laugh at our familiar joke, that it was okay to be crazy as a parent as long as only one parent was losing it at any given time. Two parents losing it and the whole house goes down. "You ready again?"

"No, but let's do this. Later I want to go check out the areas on the map."

"Sounds like a plan. Let's wrap up the calls soon and do a little drive by and hit the Wincos."

We take in one deep breath together and head upstairs like two people walking to their death. Dead parents walking, move aside. We don't even get to the top landing before he's ready to go again. "I'm going to head down to Oregon to check the mall areas. Bio Dad has been taking her to the malls down there, maybe I'll spot her. I'm going to drive through the 99th & 99th Winco too on the way down. I'll go nuts if I stay here."

"K. I'll call with any leads and you can check them out." I know he won't be able to sit still long enough to make the necessary calls.

Gary agrees and heads out again. He checks in as he crosses into Portland. We live just a short distance from the border of Oregon and it's where her bio father lives, so it's another hopeful lead.

12:02 p.m. Facebook message received from Paul

"Mary may come home if she can keep using drugs. We are still negotiating." I share with Gary their news. Gary and I agree, there will be no negotiating with Sam. She won't be continuing her behavior. Period.

12:14 p.m. Facebook message received from Sienna

"Hi I'm Sienna, I'm one of Sam's close friends. She did not tell me she left or ran away but I texted her. Told her I'd do anything to know where she is and if she's safe. I said I wouldn't tell anyone but that's a lie because we need her home. I need her home and so do you. Do you want us to put out flyers for her? I used to live in Ridgefield, I now live in Vancouver by Fort."

Without knowing it, I had just received contact from the person who would be the most instrumental in getting Samantha back.

Gary calls. "I'm at the Lloyd Center Mall. No sign of her. Any leads come in?"

"One of her classmates said she talked about some stuff she bought at Mall 205. Maybe there? It's a long shot, though."

"I know, but it's something to do. I'll call when I get there."

I continue with my calls as Gary checks in by phone every ten minutes or so. He calls from Mall 205.

"No sign of her. Now where should I look?"

"What about Clackamas Town Center?" I'm not from Oregon and

don't know all the malls in the city, but Clackamas is well known. It hit national news in December 2012 when they had a mall shooter incident there. Gary's sister had been in the mall at the time and had escaped with the crowd, and it had removed my own desire to ever shop there again. None of us had been back to the mall since then, opting for closer options, but today seemed like as good a day as any to change that streak.

"Clackamas, huh? I suppose that's a good one to try. I'll give it a try and call you. That will make a circle of malls down here."

"You're driving in circles; that seems appropriate today."

I hang up and wipe my dry erase board clean. I put "11:30 p.m. jumps" on the top. I begin to jot down what we know, what we've learned and verified as much as we could, and I start to try and build a timeline of where she could have gone. With no ID, no money, and no parent I doubt she can travel too far. *But that would be on her own. They have her, and they probably handle those issues all the time. Okay, so that's out as a deterrent.* I realize the problem is that with sex trafficking she could literally be halfway around the globe and I wouldn't know it. I'd never know it. The fear begins to creep in. *What if we never find her? What if we never see her again? Or even know what happened to her? What if this is how it works...that one day you have a child and one day they have her. Period, your time is over and you were never even asked. Thanks for raising a beautiful daughter, I think I'll just take her now.* The insult and disrespect their actions have on us is mind-boggling and I sit there taking it in. These people who never met us decided our girl was theirs. I shake my head but I still can't take the concept in. It flies in the face of everything I believe in as a parent. And what about the girls? They think they have this great boyfriend and wind up being sold? It's cruel on multiple levels and wrapping my head around it is impossible right now.

12:25 p.m. Email received from Anna

"Hi Diane, I'm someone who hangs out at the skate park and I thought you should know there's a guy that's always down there with Sammy. He gives her things all the time. Make-up, clothes, her phone.

His name is Higgs. He's not a good person. I thought you should know." I respond asking her for more information, but I never hear from her again.

I add ecigs, pot, alcohol, and place to stay under the heading "bio dad." I add phone, clothes, makeup, etc. under the heading "park pimp boy." Some things are getting cleared up and it's good to be able to stand back and look at the board to see where I should go next with the search. In looking at it, though, what I see is a young lady who was manipulated by some very slimy men. Her bio dad should have been protecting her, not buying her ecigs and letting her have sex in his apartment. *Her park pimp boy should have found another girl; he messed with one that has a lioness as a mom. Idiot. I'm going to ruin his life. I'm going to ruin all their lives.*

HOUR 14:

Hello, Sienna

12:30-1:30 p.m.

12:34 p.m. Facebook message response to Sienna

"Sienna, thank you, that would be great."

12:34 p.m. Facebook message received from Sienna

"Okay, I really wanna see her get home safe. I knew she has been sneaking out and she would tell me everything. But I was trying to help her and stop doing the things she was. She said she wanted to change but she likes the rush of going to parties. I tried helping, idk. I don't wanna see her hurt or even worse. I just want her home safe."

I send her a quick response that I agree completely and would be willing to do anything to get Sam safe. *She would tell me everything. Good to know. Hello, new friend Sienna. Let's get to know each other....*

12:39 p.m. Facebook message received from Aria

"I've shared this in Longview and put you on our prayer chain."

I'm grateful to have it shared up north where Sam's bio mom lives. It increases our exposure and the number of eyes on Sam. And again I'm touched to know our family is on another prayer chain.

Every one of those notifications makes me smile, and those are very welcome today.

12:40 p.m. Facebook message received from Mark.

He sends me a copy of a Snapchat message between two girls discussing Sam. One of them mentions seeing her at Vancouver Mall and that her hair was red. I message him back a thank you but receive no further information from him.

Gary calls; he's been driving around the Clackamas Town Center but can't find her. I'm not surprised. "Where should I head now? Any leads?"

"I just got a tip that she could be in the Vancouver Mall area."

"I'm on my way. Keep me posted. Do we know what area of the mall?"

"No further information right now. I'm working the teens and trying to get more info. I'll call if I do."

I message a few of the teens back to see if any have heard she's at Vancouver Mall. It has gotten strangely quiet on social media given that her missing post is up to 300 shares.

*Sam's Notes: My friends had started messaging and texting me about Mom's messages to them. I had seen her posts and knew she was calling everyone I knew. I messaged everyone to shut up.

I receive a call from Roy. The arrest warrant is going in now.

1:07 p.m. Arrest warrant filed and issued

I call Gary and let him know the warrant has been issued. As soon as we find her, we have a secured place to put her.

"How will you get her to stay in the Jeep while you get her there?"

"I called Tim. He's standing by and will hold her in the back seat if need be. He won't let her out."

I'm grateful to Gary's friend Tim. Sam had grown up with Tim being in her life. Tim's a tall man, a few heads and shoulders taller than any of us, and Sam had connected with him when she was just a little child. They would bump fists and joke around, and the friendship between this tall man and this little short girl was always heartwarming to observe. She trusted and respected him, and knowing it would be him sitting in the back with her brings me tremendous comfort. He could talk to her. I doubt she'd jump with him back there. He's a retired construction worker, so I don't worry he could hold on to her physically if need be. I hope it won't come to that, but being prepared for it is needed.

"One of her friends sent me a copy of a Snapchat. It says her hair is red now. Just FYI, she may not be our blonde Sam anymore."

"What's Snapchat?"

"A teen chat site."

"And Sam is in Snapchat?"

"I think every teen is in Snapchat. It's like their primary chat service. That and Kik."

"Kik?"

"Another teen chat site."

"Did you know she was on these sites?"

"Yes. I didn't see any harm. It kept her in social contact with her friends while she was homeschooled. I saw it as a social development tool."

"And now?"

"Still not seeing the harm. Without it I wouldn't know her hair was red now. Snapchat and Kik didn't make her run. Her life did."

We discuss what I've learned from the messages and texts about how she met these people.

"How would she even meet a pimp, Diane? I don't get it. We live in small-town USA."

"Right?! But here's what I'm gathering from the different messages. This guy Higgs showed up in the park and started chatting to the girls. He showed them attention and offered them things. However, most of the girls said no and avoided him. Sam thought he was cute and accepted the stuff. Just like the Shared Hope International website talked about, Gary. Remember, the lover-boy technique of recruitment? He was giving her stuff. Make-up, clothes, a phone."

"I thought you took her phone away from her."

"I did. I found a phone charger under her bed that doesn't fit any of our old phones, though, so I'm pretty sure she has one."

"When I was in her room last night talking to her, I kept hearing a buzzing sound. I asked her if she had a phone going off, but she said no. It kept buzzing, though, so I told her I was going to pull her bed apart until I found it."

"Did you?"

"I pulled most of it out, but didn't see anything. She said she was exhausted and just needed some sleep and if I'd just go she would go to bed and we could talk in the morning."

"I'm guessing that was her phone, provided by Higgs and paid for on her back."

"I should have tossed the rest of the bed."

"We should have done a lot of things."

We go silent as we both reflect in our own part in this mess. We have so much to repair.

"From what I'm reading, over time Higgs demanded some kind of payment for the stuff, and when Sam couldn't get the money, he demanded other payment."

"Pig. I want to rip him apart."

"I know. But the reality is, we didn't check up on her. We didn't follow up and go physically check where she was. We trusted even when we had reason not to. Before we go after him legally—legally, Gary, not physically--and we will, we need to fix this family."

"I agree with the fix family thing; I'm not sure I agree with the rest. But we aren't functioning very well, that's true."

"We don't function at all. So let's get Sam locked up and away from them, assessed so we know what she's on and how bad it is, try and get some extra lock-up time so we can figure out the after care, and hope we can bring her back from this experience."

"We have a long road ahead of us."

"We do. Let's find Sam so we can get started. No matter what they've done to her, we can bring her back. She has a lot of people praying for her right now, and she's on four prayer chains that I know of. She has a lot of power working on her behalf today."

"Let's hope it works."

"It will. It has to. There isn't another option I can entertain and still breathe."

1:21 p.m. Facebook message received from Paul-
"I sent an email with tips on locating a missing child."

As much as I appreciate this man's continued information and tips, I find it to be something I can ignore. His tips have had his daughter out there for months, and I'm not sure I want to follow that model of reclaiming my child from the streets. I want a quicker, more secure option. For the first and only time, I realize I'm grateful for her prior trouble. Without that probation violation warrant and lock-up option, we would be facing bringing Sam back to the house and having a talk with her. The truth is, that wouldn't work, and she'd run again as soon as we fell asleep. *She's going to hate me for this. Hate me. She may never forgive me or talk to me again for doing this.*

Gary tells me he's nearing the Vancouver Mall area....

HOUR 15:

Closing In...

1:30-2:30 p.m.

I hate the waiting. I can tell from Gary's tone and conversation that he's exhausted. He's rambling about traffic and the calls from the job site, but I'm not really listening. I'm staring out the window at a young girl riding her bike up and down the street. She's weaving back and forth, her hair blowing in the early summer wind. Her friend is laughing and running alongside her. They look so carefree. *Watch out, girls; there's a devil at the park and he'll get you too if you're not careful.* A car drives by with a young man behind the wheel and I glare at the driver, instantly suspecting him of being the pimp. *Will I ever view young men the same? Will I always suspect them all of being perverted pigs? How sad for the good ones.* I watch the car until it turns right at the corner and disappears from view. The girls return to claiming the neighborhood as their own playground and go back to riding up and down the street. Even though I know I keep watch on this block, my mind can't wrap around how many blocks are out there, unwatched, where the children are vulnerable. *Are any of us really watching our children as much as we think we are?*

Gary and I continue with small talk as he drives toward Vancouver Mall, until he gets a call from the job site. "I'll call you back."

I run through the Facebook pages of all the teens, looking for any updates or additional information. I see two more posts about people seeing her at Vancouver Mall. I don't want to get my hopes too high, but I quietly wish Gary's Jeep had wings. The sooner he gets there, the better. *We're getting closer, Sam--we're closing in on you.*

I step out back to have a smoke and now that I've got daylight, I walk around the perimeter of the house to get a good look at the roofline. I can see a few places where it would be possible, if someone was young and agile, that they could get up and down to the second story roof. From there it would be fairly easy to climb through any of the three windows on the back side of the house. And all three windows were in rooms she controlled. The guest room, the bathroom in the middle, and her hang-out room on the south side. If she left the windows unlocked, she could quite easily slip in and out without us hearing her. That part of the roof was over the sun porch; we wouldn't hear the footsteps overhead in our room. I walk around front to look at the window she jumped from. I guess that she used the small overhang, slid down that and jumped into the bush by the front door. I check around the bush and see a place where the bark dust is displaced and clumped up as if something landed on it. It's strange to stand there looking at the spot where she landed just hours ago.

I bend down and touch the center of the spot, my sad attempt at connecting to her. *Are you okay, Sam? Are you safe?* I go back to the back deck and toss my cigarette butt in the dragon. I look out over the river and marina, and take in a deep breath. For just a moment I close my eyes and enjoy being a part of the other world, the normal your-kid's-not-on-the-streets world. I go back inside, close the door, and hit the kitchen for a fresh pot of coffee. While it brews I open my iPad and shoot a message to Sienna. I need to get this girl responding to me and decide to get a bit more hardline with her. One of the forwarded Snapchat messages said Sam had been hanging out with Sienna for a while, which was news to me, but meant she could know more than she was telling me.

2:05 p.m. Facebook message sent to Sienna

"Sienna we still have no word. Mary's dad hooked Sam's dad up with national organizations and this is turning huge really quick. The outcome for Sammy is getting worse by the hour. The very best thing she can do is go turn herself in to the juvenile department. The cops have been warned not to mistreat her worked-on shoulder, but I can't guarantee her safety until she starts to use that brain. We've been filled in on some of her activities lately. We know she's been sneaking out at night, selling herself for money, stealing, dealing ecstasy, and ruining her family... Have I missed anything? The more we know the more likely we are to find her..."

While most of what I tell this teen is true, I don't hesitate to stretch the legal consequences to put a little scare in her for Sam's sake. All of her friends know about Sam's shoulder reconstruction and are protective over her disability. By mentioning possible police rough handling of Sam's shoulder, I hope to tap into Sienna's protective nature over Sam. It works.

2:08 p.m. Facebook message received from Sienna

"Doing molly and possibly coke I once went to a party with her to make sure nothing happened to her because the people that went she didn't know very well, I didn't either but I didn't want her getting hurt. I tried to help her and I've done this stuff, I don't want her to do the same, I've ran away with a guy and it was good for him as for me but I've changed and I certainly don't want Sam doing this because it will hurt her future."

It takes me a read or two to decipher some of the teen talk. Somewhere in the back of my mind I am shaking my head and making disgusted noises at the spelling, grammar, and general state of American education these days.

2:10 p.m. Facebook message sent to Sienna

"What's molly? And yes, when you run with a guy it's always good for him... I wish you girls would realize that and quit undervaluing your beautiful selves. The future does not hold some dude who encouraged you to leave your family. It just doesn't."

Sienna grows quiet and I worry she's gone. I receive a text from my friend D.W., letting me know he's praying for me and including some scriptures to read for peace. His message reminds me to take a moment to pray. *Lord, I come to you humbled as a parent. I pray you lend me your strength. I'm battling harsh enemies here today, and I'm doing it with a broken heart. Heal me, Lord; heal me so I can do what I need to. Let the right ears hear my cries, let the right eyes see my words, let the right people help us on our journey. Amen.* I sit and just breathe in and out for a minute. *He's got this.*

2:13 p.m. Facebook message received from Sienna

"But yes that's probably the reason she left was with some guys."

My heart jumps at the ping of the message received notice. I'm relieved she's still with me.

2:14 p.m. Facebook message sent to Sienna

"Well, she's gone down a path only she can repair. Her probation officer already had a warrant issued for her arrest. He pushed it through due to the stories from her friend's dad on her activities. They are calling in sex trafficking organizations now."

2:15 p.m. Facebook message received from Sienna

"I know she's been selling herself for money for some guy, I don't want that to be the reason she's missing, I won't be able to deal with her being hurt from sex trafficking or worse."

2:16 p.m. Facebook message sent to Sienna

"So she has a pimp, basically."

2:16 p.m. I post on Facebook

"No updates :(" Even a basic post keeps the story fresh and bumped to the top of people's updates. Anything that keeps her missing poster being shared and seen is a plus. Her share count tops 500.

2:17 p.m. Facebook message received from Sienna

"Yea she said she did stuff with guys for money for a guy and I said me and her needed to talk because I won't let her do that stuff but she said she didn't want anyone to hurt her if she told the guy she didn't want to do it anymore. She never named names."

My heart breaks reading this. *She didn't want anyone to hurt her. She's afraid of this guy.* The mother lioness in me began to claw at my insides and screamed for this man's blood. *How dare he scare her into this?* The need to find her increases with every message this girl sends me. I decide to risk pushing her a little harder.

2:19 p.m. Facebook message sent to Sienna

"She's crafty. Well, anyone with her that's helping her will be arrested for aiding a runaway. And she'll be arrested because her probation officer ordered it and got it signed by the judge this morning. There's not much that can be done to help her. There are so many people out wasting their time looking for her. She doesn't want to be found, she won't be. Do you have a name for this guy, or where she meets him, his car make...anything can help." I want to keep her off balance in the conversation, nervous for her own trouble if she helps Sam, and hit with questions while her brain is occupied. I already know his name is Higgs, but I play dumb in case she divulges another name.

2:20 p.m. Facebook message received from Sienna

"Higgs. I texted her, she has a Facebook and I made it sound like I won't tell you where she is, I will, I won't have her doing this, I've done this and it hurt me and my family."

I have what I consider to be final confirmation of the pimp's name. I guess I needed to hear it from a few people. Higgs. It's weird to have a name. *Satan has a name, it's Higgs.*

2:23 p.m. Facebook message received from Paul

"I've sent an email with how to make a poster and the benefits of a disposable search phone." I truly appreciate the help and support this man is sending, but I don't bother to reply.

I go for really laying on some parental guilt on the teens following this thread on Facebook.

2:25 p.m. I post to my Facebook page

"But there is NOTHING that can ever prepare you for the sounds your husband makes when his daughter is missing... Nothing. That is raw."

I wait to see if Sienna responds to my post. The clock ticks as people comment on it, but I don't see Sienna liking or commenting on it. *I hope she reads it.*

2:26 p.m. Facebook notification

Sienna liked your post.

2:27 p.m. Facebook message sent to Sienna

"I'm dying here. Her father is losing it. This was too much. He is crying his lungs out downstairs...please help us, Sienna."

The truth is that Gary isn't even home. But I don't want this girl to know we are moving Gary into position at the mall. If that's where Sam is, I don't want her being tipped off. I want Sienna, who has quickly become our best bet at locating Sam, to feel our pain. I want her desperate to help us.

2:28 p.m. Facebook message received from Sienna

"I'm trying, I really am." Her words sound so familiar to me; they are what Sammy mutters every time her grades slip. "I'm trying, I really am." Only she hadn't been trying. Would this girl actually try to help, or would her promises of help be like Samantha's promises of good behavior and grades? *How did I wind up depending on the rationale of a teenager to save Sam?*

HOUR 16:

There's No Air...There's No Air.

2:30-3:30 p.m.

As I sit and wait for Gary to be in position, for Sienna to call, for more leads to come in, I notice a lack of air. I'm trying to breathe, but it doesn't seem to make much difference; I still feel like passing out. Every minute is torture. My eyes dart from phone to iPad to window. Phone to iPad to window. Over and over again, waiting for a break. Waiting for a ping, a notice, anything to indicate we are moving in the right direction. Phone to iPad to window, phone to iPad to window. The phone rings--it's Gary. I snatch it up and answer, "Yes, any news?"

"No I was hoping you had some. I'm at the mall, driving around. I don't see her."

"All signs point to her being in the area. What side of the mall are you on?"

"I'm down by Sears. I'll drive around by Macy's and around the corner to the other side. No sign of her though, blonde or redhead."

2:54 p.m. Facebook message received from Sienna

"Sam texted me. She's at the Vancouver Mall. She was just turned out. Me and my mom are on our way to get her."

2:54 p.m. Call to Gary

"She's at Vancouver Mall, Gary. Sienna just verified it. Her and her mom are on their way to get her."

"What are they driving? Where are they meeting her?"

"I don't have any more info than that--I'll keep you posted."

2:50 p.m. Email from Sue

Still nothing at Winco, Momma."

2:54 p.m. Facebook message received from Leah

"Hi I know you don't know who I am or maybe you may have heard of me from years and years ago. Peter is like Sammy's little brother and we live here in Ridgefield and Sammy contacted me on Saturday and wanted me to take her to Vancouver but I wasn't in Ridgefield so I couldn't take her. Peter and I are down at Abrams Park. Peter's walking the trails looking in the trees or anything to see if maybe she might be down there I'm trying to help as much as I can. Trust me it's breaking my heart to know that she's out there I want to let you know that if you need anybody to talk to you or anything please contact me I live right in Ridgefield too so I will help do whatever I can to try to find her."

I don't know who this lady is, but she sure seems to know my child. The name Peter seems familiar, but I can't remember right in the middle of the Sienna messages why that name is under my skin.

3:00 p.m. Facebook message received from Sienna

"I'm headed to Vancouver Mall with my mom."

3:01 p.m. Call to Gary

"Sienna and her mom just left for the mall. They should be there in a few minutes. Drive around and keep your eyes open. Sam is contacting Sienna, so I know she's there. Somewhere, she's there somewhere."

"I'll just keep circling the mall parking lot until I hear from you."

"Sounds good; I'll keep working this girl and try and get a car make or address."

"We may be close, Diane. We may actually get her back."

"I don't want to get my hopes up, but yes, I feel it too. We're close."

"If I see her I'm throwing it into park, leaving the door open, grabbing her and literally throwing her in the car and taking off."

"These people could be nearby, Gary. You should figure they're watching her. They won't let their property go without a fight. I'm worried."

"Don't be. There is no man on this planet that will dare to try and stop me from putting her in the Jeep. God help them if they try."

"Once you have her, straight to juvenile detention?"

"Yep. I won't pass go, won't collect $200, straight to lock-up so we can figure out what's happened."

"Gary, thank you. Thank you for being out there, for being ready to grab her."

"We're GOING to get through this Diane. Trust."

We agree I'll stay on the Facebook messages and call him with any further developments. Otherwise he'll continue driving a loop around the mall until further notice.

3:09 p.m. Facebook message received from Leah

"Carla said that Sammy messaged her last night and said she was going to run away. And claims she is going to go across country like her mom told her to." I wish all these kids who had concerns and prior knowledge this was going to happen would have picked up the phone and let one of us know.

3:10 p.m. Call to Gary

I share with him the message from Leah and the news from Carla. Gary calls Carla while he's driving the mall parking lot to try and get more information from her.

3:15 p.m. Call from Gary

"I can't stand that little witch. I'm so glad they aren't friends anymore!"

"What did Carla have to say?"

Carla and Sam had been friends for years, more like sisters. Carla was as comfortable in our home as Sam was at hers. Although I found her mom to be rather irritating, I enjoyed Carla and found their friendship touching. Until the trouble with the pills came up. Sam had given Carla the stolen pills at her home and Carla had taken them to school and sold them. Carla's mom had called me and lectured me on raising teenagers. I had successfully turned two adults out in to the world while she had yet to turn a single one out as a success, but she felt I needed her sage advice on raising children. I had listened patiently, but secretly couldn't wait to see how she was going to handle turning out Carla, who had slut tendencies. The girl flipped from boy to boy, had been caught having sex in her bedroom multiple times, and always thought she was pregnant. I don't think there was a single time she spent the night that she didn't spend time on the phone with her mom trying to calm the woman down. Her mom would call screaming about what she saw as Carla's latest offense, and I would spend time after the calls comforting the crying teen. The two fought constantly and Carla spoke often of how much she couldn't wait to be grown so she could get away from that woman.

Carla's mom had been the most vocal in proclaiming her child's innocence at the high school when the trouble happened. Even after the video clearly showing Carla selling the pills was shown to her, she still denied it. She claimed Sam was the bad influence on her daughter and had forbidden all contact between the girls forever. It had hurt Sam deeply, but she hoped she and Carla could have a friendship when they both turned eighteen and Carla wasn't living with her mom anymore.

"Why, didn't she have anything to say that could help us? If they've been in contact, then Carla knows something."

"Oh, she knows something, but her only response to me was 'Sorry Gary, I WON'T get involved in this.'"

"She won't?! Does she get that Sam, her bestie up until a few months ago, could be sold?! She has nothing to say to help?"

"No, she's as weak as always. I can't stand her, Diane. She was so smug on the phone, like she had the answers and screw us."

"I can't believe she wouldn't help. Do you think she'd talk if I asked her?"

"Nope. She was real clear, we are not to contact her again, ask her any questions, or come to her for help. Sam is on her own. Those were her words--Sam is on her own because she'll be in trouble with her mom if she finds out she's been talking to Sam. What a great quality friend."

"What a sad pathetic little human being. Fine, we'll do it without her."

"Scum."

"Right? She is. Let's be grateful she's in our daughter's past, and after this, forever will be."

"If anything happens to Sam and she's been sitting on information, I want to sue her, or press charges, or do something to ruin her miserable little life." Gary is usually such a calm person--I'm a little taken back by his anger toward Carla, but I can understand it.

I'd like to show up in her door and break her scrawny little neck. The anger I feel at this girl who has information but is unwilling to share it to protect herself is indescribable. She would rather Sam die on the streets than risk being in trouble with her mom for talking to Sam. *Coward.* I realize given a dark road and no witnesses, it's very likely I would run her over, back up, and run her over again. I've never wanted to choke someone as badly as I wanted to choke the information out of this self-centered traitor to our family. Again I have to stop and remember my Bible lessons. I find it difficult to hold on to my new beliefs in the face of so many horrid people hurting my child. Gary and I agree that regardless of the outcome, this girl will never be welcome in our home again. She's done. I take a deep breath and try and practice forgiveness, but knowing she could help and won't is too much for me right now.

"So now where are you?"

"North side by the old theater. I simply don't see her, Diane. Are you sure she's here?"

"The last message from Sienna said that's where she was. They had just turned her out to do business."

"I'll drive around the front again. Sam, where are you?" Gary sounds frustrated, but I feel like we're close. Like any minute she'll step out in front of the Jeep and it will be over.

Any minute...

HOUR 17:

It Ends With A Fall...

3:30 p.m.-Capture

Gary continues his circle around the mall, pulling over every now and then to just watch the exits. I continue to monitor Facebook and hope to hear from Sienna soon.

3:39 p.m. Facebook message received from Wendy

"I shared this in Winlock." Even though we are closing in, I welcome all the new shares and eyes out there.

I continue to monitor the social media accounts, answer emails, and work the phones, but it's obvious this girl Sienna is in a position to help us. Waiting for her to respond is killing me, though. Every minute that passes without word from her is an eternity.

4:00 p.m. Facebook response to Sienna

"Is everything okay?" Any word from this girl would be a relief.

4:00 p.m. Facebook response sent to Leah

"She's referring to her biological mother. We hear she's in Portland near a mall with a man named Higgs. That's he's her pimp. Do you know anything from this that can help? We are desperate. We're not bad parents,

I don't care what she says. We just want her safe. She doesn't have to live here if it's that bad. But a pimp?! I can't handle that. I can't."

4:01 p.m. Facebook message received from Leah

"I kind of figured that's who she was referring to all the things I know right now is she told me she was okay she won't tell me where she is. She contacted Carla last night and said that she was going to go cross country like I told you. I just talked to her bio Dad. We should talk. She's by some mall with some guy I don't know. I have talked to the Ridgefield police and given them the information I do have. If I come up with anything else or find out anything or she will let me come get her I will let you guys know before anything else happens." With everything happening with Sienna, the words this woman just sent me don't register until later. I read it quickly and will use her for backup if I need it.

4:02 p.m. Facebook message received from Leah

"She's never said anything bad about you guys ever and you know the couple times I have seen her in town she seems so happy. Her posts on Facebook she's making dinner for the family she seems happy I don't understand this at all."

4:02 p.m. Facebook message received from Sienna

"She's with me but can we have like 30 minutes so I can talk to her?"

Relief. There are no words to adequately speak the relief I feel. *She's with me. She's with me.* She's not on the streets, she's not sold and gone, she's with Sienna. Such wonderful words were just spoken to me.

4:02 p.m. Call to Gary

"They have her! They have her! She's with Sienna and her mom, oh Gary, they have her!" The tears are streaming down my face and I'm so relieved to feel like we are one step from having her secured.

"What are they in? Did you get a car make yet? What side of the mall are they on?" Gary sounds desperate and is practically screaming at me.

"I don't know; I'm trying to find out. But they have her Gary, they have her!"

"I know Diane, but **we** don't. We're not there yet."

I sniffle back my excitement and settle down; he's right, **we** don't have her yet.

4:03 p.m. Facebook message sent to Sienna

"Yes thank you! What kind of car are you in?"

Gary is on the phone asking me if she's responded, and I'm refreshing my Facebook page every few seconds in case she has, but no word.

"Can you look this girl up on the web, Diane? Can you search out her address like you do on other people?"

"I can try, Gary. I'll call you back in a few minutes if I get lucky."

I plug what I know about this girl into my search programs and start trying to track down where she might live. If she goes quiet, we aren't any better off than when we started.

4:08 p.m. Facebook message received from Sienna

"She's at my house." The notification ping and message throw my heart into racing speed. *Here we go....*

4:08 p.m. Facebook response to Sienna

"What's your address, Sienna?" I hold my breath. *Will she give it to me? Am I about to get the address of where Sam is?*

4:09 p.m. Facebook message received from Sienna

"Don't come right now please let me talk to her. My address is: 3810 Mondon lane. Me and her are going on a walk imma talk to her." *Omg I have the address of where Sam is!*

4:09 p.m. Call to Gary.

"I have the address! I'm plugging it into Google now." Because Gary insists on using a flip phone, he has no access to handy modern phone features like mapping or GPS. This requires me to be his internet and relay the information as I receive it.

Lesson Learned: None; Gary still loves his flip phone.

"Where am I headed?"

"3810 Mondon Lane. It's over by the Parsely Center. Where Sam took homeschool PE in 7th grade."

"I'll head to that neighborhood, you plug it in to Google so you can lead me in."

I plug the address in, but it looks like it's a small lane and could be difficult to locate. I describe the entrance to Gary. He can't locate it and starts circling the block. I plug it back into Google but it still shows the entrance where I'm telling him. "Let me call the cops and get them going over there. I'll call you back." I don't wait for a response but hang up and dial 911.

"This is Diane Geister. There is a warrant for my daughter and I've just discovered the address of where she is. Can I get a car over there to pick her up please?"

The operator takes the address down and says they'll send a car as soon as they can.

I call Gary back. "The cops are sending a car that way. Did you find the street entrance?"

"No, I'm making one more swing around the block. I don't know where Google is seeing this street, but I'm not."

I can't believe after all this, it's coming down to finding a small lane entrance. I describe in detail where Google shows the entrance, and drop down to street level so I can describe what I'm seeing. "It's there, Gary, you HAVE to find it."

"I'm hanging up so I can concentrate. I'll call you when I find it." He hangs up suddenly and I go back to working Sienna.

4:18 p.m. I post an update to Facebook

"Not yet...closing in. I'm holding my breath."

I hope Sienna is seeing the post, and realizing every second is killing me. I wait and watch to see if she likes it, or responds. Nothing.

Gary calls, he found the street. "I don't think that qualifies as a street. It looks like a driveway with one tiny little sign hidden behind a tree. That took me forever."

"Are you there now? Outside her house?"

"Yes. I'm backed up just outside her gate. She won't get by me." I breathe a tiny sigh of relief--Gary is just feet away from her now!

4:23 p.m. Facebook message received from Sienna

"Text me when you gonna come."

"I just got a Facebook message from her, Gary. Do you want me to tell her you're there already?"

"Hang on--I got out to look around a bit, see what I'm up against. Give me a few minutes. I want to check out where to hide. Are the cops coming?"

"They say they are. I'll call them real quick and call you back."

I call the police. They tell me there's a car heading down that way.

I call Gary back. "Car on its way. Should we delay trying to capture her and let them handle it?"

"If we can. I'm not waiting, though. They'll need to hurry."

The phone rings and I put Gary on hold. It's the police. They're not finding a warrant on file for Samantha.

"It's there. Roy put it through this afternoon. We're snagging her in a few minutes and bringing her in to juvenile. We need that warrant to hold her. Where's the warrant?!"

"We'll contact Roy and get back to you, ma'am. But in the meantime the officers won't be able to intervene in this matter." They hang up and I immediately dial Roy. It goes to voicemail. "Roy, it's Diane. Where's Sam's warrant? I'm trying to get her picked up and the cops are saying there's no warrant. I need that warrant, Roy! Call me back please!"

I switch back to Gary. "What's going on, Diane?"

"They can't find her warrant, so the cops can't come pick her up."

"Are you telling me we've located her and they won't come get her because they screwed up and don't have the warrant ready?!"

"Yes, that's exactly what I'm telling you. It's up to us, Gary. Grab her anyway."

"Oh, I will, but then what?!"

"You grab her and I'll work the warrant end. I'm telling Sienna you're there."

4:34 p.m. Facebook response to Sienna

"Her dad is outside waiting outside of your fence."

"I've let her know you're out there, Gary."

"I found a great place to tuck in by the gate exit. The Jeep can't be seen and I'll be able to grab her pretty easily I think."

4:34 p.m. Facebook message received from Sienna

"I need to talk to her still."

4:34 p.m. Facebook response to Sienna

"He's not leaving." *Not a chance!*

4:34 p.m. Facebook message received from Sienna-

"You said half an hour."

4:35 p.m. Facebook response to Sienna

"He isn't doing more than waiting for you to text me. And it was half an hour."

This girl is making me nervous. Come on, Sienna, get Sam out that gate. Just get her out the gate.

4:35 p.m. Facebook message received from Sienna

"Okay… so don't tell Sam I set her up please, say you tracked her phone because I can't loose her. And okay hold on she's in the bathroom."

The police call. I throw Gary on hold again. There is no warrant on record. If we bring her to juvenile detention, they won't hold her. I desperately try and explain our situation to the bored-sounding clerk, but the message is the same. No warrant...no hold.

4:36 p.m. Facebook response to Sienna

"Do what you need to just get her to her dad. I think he backed up out of view."

I call Roy again and beg him to respond about the warrant.

4:37 p.m. Facebook message received from Sienna

"Okay. We're about to walk down the driveway, so be ready."

"Gary, they're coming out now!"

"I'm putting my phone on the Jeep seat face up so you can hear, but I want my hands free, Diane. Okay?"

"Whatever works--just get her, Gary. Please don't let her get by you!"

"I won't, Diane--I promise you I won't."

4:41 p.m. Facebook response to Sienna

"Okay, he should be there."

4:41 p.m. I email Pat, the director of all Juvenile Services

"Pat, this is Diane Geister, your ex-student. Samantha and her dad Gary are headed to your detention center. They will be turned away. She was listed as a runaway this morning, has a pimp, involved in sex trafficking. Her PO Roy talked to me this morning and claimed he got a warrant signed for her. No one can find it anywhere nor reach him. Please lock her up. Please, or she'll run. This is ridiculous he would lie about a warrant and then fail to respond to calls all day from multiple people. They are going to be there any minute... Please HELP! Diane Geister." I include my phone number, title it URGENT URGENT URGENT, and hope for the best.

There is no air in this room. I'm trying to suck in a breath, but my chest is squeezed in a vice. My head is swimming, my chest is doing strange convulsive movements, but there's no air going in me. Where's the air?!

"She's coming--I have to be ready," Gary whispers into the phone before dropping it on the driver's seat of his Jeep. Everything goes quiet and still, and then screaming. I can hear Samantha in the background shouting at her dad and him yelling back. There is the sound of feet running past the Jeep and multiple people all shouting.

"What's happening?" I scream, but no one is close enough to answer. "What's happening?!" I scream it over and over again. "Someone answer me, oh please someone answer me."

My heart feels like it's barely beating as the tears flow down my face. At least I know she's in his sight. At least she's alive! *Thank you God.* I cry openly as the last seventeen hours wash over me. *She is alive. She is alive!* My breath is ragged and the tears flow as I wait for what seems an endless amount of time for someone to update me. *Had he caught her? Had she slipped away? Was the pimp there? Would Gary be safe? Oh please, Lord, oh please let them be safe.*

More noises and shouting as I hear the door of the Jeep open. The phone is jostled and I start screaming for someone to talk to me. "Do you have her, do you have her?" I scream it over and over again until I hear Gary's voice on the other end of the line.

4:44 p.m. Facebook message received from Sienna
"For her."

4:45 p.m.
Gary says the most beautiful words ever spoken to the mom of a missing child: "I have her."

No words have stood out more since his words seventeen hours earlier when he said she jumped. *I have her.* Those three words unlock the floodgates and I sob uncontrollably in absolute relief.

EPILOGUE

The Days After

*Sam's Notes: I was not expecting Dad to be hiding outside Sienna's gate. I had no idea I had been set up. I honestly thought I could outrun him.

*Gary's Notes: Sam saw me and bolted down the road. Sienna and her mom were screaming for Samantha to stop, but that kid took off. I chased her down and she tried to cut through some bramble bushes. I jumped and tackled her, knocking her down to the ground. I grabbed her arm and held it in a death grip until I had physically dragged her back to the Jeep. With Sienna on one side I put Sam in the middle and her mom jumped in to sandwich her in between. I may be sixty, but I can still outrun and take down a sixteen-year-old!

Sienna and her mom rode down to the juvenile detention center with Gary and Sam to keep her from running. The warrant was located in the system and waiting for them by the time they arrived. It was explained to me that a warrant can be filed, but that everyone having it in their hands takes a little time. Sigh. Samantha was locked up and court set for the next morning.

5/26, 6:44 p.m. Facebook message sent to Sienna

"There are no words of gratitude to send your way for your work today, Sienna. After two days up we will sleep tonight knowing she is at least safe. Court tomorrow morning. We are just wiped from this. Thank you again and again, and your mom."

The days following Samantha's capture became a surreal world of court appointments, jail visits, assessments, and a mad scramble to line up her after care.

5/27, 9:00 a.m. Court.

Sam entered with hair the color of Raggedy Ann's hair. I made sure she saw me looking at it, and I smirked. I told the bailiff if he wanted to shave it all off before sending her home, I'd be okay with that. Sam made a quick appearance and had an attorney appointed to her. She was given three days on a first-time probation violation. She barely looked at me and we didn't touch or talk at all.

5/28, 10:55 p.m. Facebook message sent to Sienna

"Sienna I invite you to come to court tomorrow morning at 9 a.m. I'm inviting all of her relatives. I'm going to tell her her community loves her enough until she loves herself enough. We are shooting for long-term rehab with counseling. We hired her lifetime counselor and she's going to do Sam's assessment in jail. Sam loves her and trusts her. We almost have her rehab locked down, and tomorrow will ask for some more time to get it nailed down so she goes straight to rehab from jail. And we'll move and fix everything in her world that has caused this. What bugged her the most? What did she want us to change?"

5/28, 10:56 p.m. Facebook message received from Sienna

"I think she didn't like that you never let her have as much freedom as she wanted."

5/29, 7:00 a.m. Facebook message sent to Sienna

"Oh, well lol. Of course not. When your grades are terrible, your room is trashed, none of your laundry is done, and your attitude bites.... Freedom never comes first. Bummer. Anything else she complained about? I'd love to make this good for her."

Sienna never responded back. I don't think my response was what she expected. I will never drop my expectations on my children to handle the basics just because they don't like them. When you are under eighteen, your job is to go to school and do your best, keep your room from collecting bugs and vermin, and pitch in when needed. It's not too difficult to meet the expectations around our home. So when I heard that Samantha was unhappy because she didn't get to have even more freedom than she was already enjoying without earning it, I had to laugh.

5/30, 9:00 a.m. Court.

I stood next to Sam when she faced the judge, and I explained our efforts at securing Sam lock-up rehab. I described the hours I had spent on the phone locating her the best after care I could find. I told Samantha that we loved her and that we would move, we would go through counseling, we would do whatever it took to make her world right. That we just didn't want her jumping from windows anymore. Sam looked at me and I finally saw her tough shell crack. Her face crumpled and the tears slid down her cheeks. Her attorney attempted to shut me down for addressing her directly and for requesting even more time on a first-time probation violation, as we expected he'd do, but I spoke to Sam's heart about our need for her to stay put in jail while we worked to fix things.

Her attorney's face was red as he demanded I stop addressing his client, but I looked at the judge and said, "She's always been, and always will be, my daughter before she's his client." The judge got it. A box of Kleenex made the rounds from clerk to judge to district attorney the longer I spoke. I told Sam her community was here to show her love and support, that she wasn't alone, and that we loved her more than she was seeing. I told her I was already packing, that we would move like she wanted. She cried the more I told her what we were doing to correct her world. She was given an additional, and unheard-of, eight days lock-up so I could get the after care lined up. Her attorney argued it was unfair, unheard-of on a first-time violation, that they weren't a holding cell for parents looking for after care... his arguments fell on deaf ears. The judge could clearly see what I was attempting to get lined up for Sam, what I was fighting against in doing so. Sam and I hugged before she left the courtroom, much to her attorney's dismay, and I let her know one more time that we loved her and would work to make things right. Her attorney was still arguing the touching we did as she was led into the back area. She raised her hand in the "I love you" sign, I made mine in return, and we stood there with the safety glass between us, an entire courtroom silent, as we connected through sign. We have love, she would be okay. She stood behind that glass, hand holding up the thumb, pointer and pinky fingers, staring at me, and I knew she was finding strength in my sign back. She had my love, I wasn't going anywhere, she hadn't chased me off.

As I went to gather my things and leave, the parents sitting behind me stood up and shook my hand. The father said this was their first time and he had no idea what to do in court or what to say when it was their turn. He did now and he thanked me for setting the example. Every parent ahead of me had stood to the back, kept quiet, didn't ask questions, and just let the system carry their child along. I told that father what I used to tell the truancy parents and the CASA parents: Stand up for your babies in court. Speak. Be aware, be a part of the solution, and speak up. What do they need? See to it they get it. No one will be a better advocate for your child in the system than you will be. Period.

Sam's after care was approved one hour before her release from detention. One hour. It was another sweat-it-out, mad-phone-calling kind of morning, but the after care was lined up and Gary and Tim picked Sam up at jail and drove her to Oregon to rehab. Her feet never touched open ground between capture and the day she was released from rehab, July 11th. By then she was clean, counseled, we had gone through communication therapy as a family, and we had a new place lined up in a town forty minutes north. Sam returned to our home for the final two weeks to help us get moved, and happily set about creating a new life for herself in her new town. She became a great student, found a job, quickly became a go-to worker, and still maintains her life as she knows she needs to.

After rehab Sam entered into long-term counseling in our new town with a wonderful counselor recommended by Mr. Bruce. What a wonderful contact he became, setting mouths to talking when he showed up in rehab to personally check on Sam. He did this a few times over the summer, making sure she had everything she needed to succeed. The staff had never known him to come in personally, so his arrival created quite the stir. I called him during the summer to update him, and I told him I would lose his number after she was better. Mr. Bruce told me he hopes I never lose his number and hopes that I'll continue to update him on Sam's progress. I'm forever grateful to this man for going outside of the box to make things happen for Sam.

I eventually put together who Leah was--the ex-girlfriend to the bio dad, and living right in town with us. I had no idea Sam had been going over to their home, playing with her son, and connecting with her bio dad through this contact. I hadn't heard of this woman for a decade and still don't know how she managed to get so close to my child without my knowing.

I finally gave up smoking after forty years. It was all part of our fresh start in our new town. I hope that my example to Sam for the rest of her childhood here at home will be a better one. I also gave up my video game, turning the entire clan and my accounts over to other players and deleting the app.

By the end of July our family had moved to our new town, gotten Sam registered at her local high school, and worked hard to keep communication good between us. Are we perfect at it? No, but our eyes and our communication are open now, and that's more than we used to have.

After months of prayer, I was able to finally find forgiveness for the people involved in this. Samantha never would name names, claiming she knew I would go after the people until I had ruined their lives, so holding on to my hatred served no good purpose. My forgiveness included the pig who attacked Sam in our home. That was probably the most difficult thing I've done as a new believer. It required some in-depth prayer, but by the time D.W. was done, I was crying with complete forgiveness for these people in my heart. He had to drag out every scripture on forgiveness, and it was still difficult to do. How do you forgive thugs for attacking your child? How do you forgive them for turning your child out? My hats off to David West for praying with me until I found forgiveness for them. What a relief to release the hatred! I hold no grudges, for I don't know them, and I don't know where on their journey with God they are. I simply couldn't judge them. Jesus gave me a new start and forgiveness, and I was compelled to pay it forward by doing the same for them. A heavy dark feeling left me the minute I truly forgave them.

Legally the men involved were already high on the police radar as traffickers and drug dealers. Our information was added to the growing pile of evidence the police were collecting on them. Eventually their crimes will catch up to them, and they'll be put away.

Samantha entered 11th grade this past fall. She loves her new school and friends. We adjusted how she gets permission for going out, using a curfew method instead of minute-by-minute micromanagement of where she is. It requires we trust her, and that's difficult after our years with Sam. But like every parent out there, we trust because we have to. A child won't develop properly without it.

So we take a deep breath, we trust our new communication tools, and we open the door for her now, because it beats watching her jump out of a window.

Sources

NCMEC. National Center for Missing and Exploited Children. **www.missingkids.org**. Index. 2016.

NHTRC. The National Human Trafficking Reaource Center. **www.traffickingresourcenter.org**. 2016.

Polly Klaas. Polly Klaas Foundation. **www.pollyklaas.org** 2016.

Shared Hope. **www.sharedhope.org**. FAQ's. 2016.

Resources

Shared Hope International.
www.sharedhope.org
Shared Hope International is dedicated to bringing an end to sex trafficking through our three-pronged approach – prevent, restore, and bring justice.

The National Human Trafficking Resource Center.
www.traffickingresourcecenter.org
The National Human Trafficking Resource Center (NHTRC) is a national anti-trafficking hotline and resource center serving victims and survivors of human trafficking and the anti-trafficking community in the United States. The toll-free hotline is available to answer calls from anywhere in the country, 24 hours a day, 7 days a week, every day of the year in more than 200 languages.

The National Center for Missing and Exploited Children.
www.missingkids.org
The National Center for Missing & Exploited Children® is the nation's clearinghouse for issues involving missing and exploited children. NCMEC provides free services and resources to, law enforcement, families and the professionals who serve them to assist in the recovery of missing children and prevent child sexual exploitation.

Polly Klaas Foundation.
www.pollyklaas.org
The Polly Klaas® Foundation is a Petaluma, CA based, national non-profit dedicated to the safety of all children, the recovery of missing children, and public policies that keep children safe in their communities.

Quick Tip Guide

- Call police and get an official report made. If there is a time requirement before the child can be reported missing, this establishes a start time.
- Turn social media notifications on. Make sure you do this for all devices.
- Call, text, or email all contacts. The more eyes you have looking immediately the better.
- Assemble notebook of numbers, names, and log-ins. This is not the time for bedroom privacy. If they wanted privacy, they should have stayed in the home. Once you have the names and numbers, call them.
- Social media. By far the most useful tool to use. If you don't use social media, it's as easy as locating your nearest teen and having them set it up for you. Send out an email that says "I have a runaway and need help creating a Facebook announcement about it." Someone will step forward to help you with it if you need it.
- Skitch is a free download that enables you to add text and other things to pictures. Create a separate page for your missing child and then add your entire contact list to it. People may mind and complain when you add them for a party they live 1000

miles from attending, but a missing child is a different matter. By adding them they get all updates as you post them. Once you have its own page created, you can target an inexpensive ad for your county, state, region, or to young users.

- Once you've created the page and posted the picture with the missing child's information, sent out an ad and posted the page link on your main page; use it for updates and information gathering only. The goal is to get the missing child picture shared onto as many other pages as possible, as quickly as possible. After the initial posting, you need someone available round the clock to monitor it. Normally I would never recommend accepting stranger friend requests, but when you're hunting down your child, every stranger is a possible lead. It's better to accept them, find out why they're there, and unfriend them later if you need to. They can be valuable tools in your search.
- Have one person monitoring social media, one person on the street, and one on the phones if possible.
- Be polite and do not lose your cool. You need the information they may be sitting on. If you yell at them, or alienate them in any way; you lose the potential leads.
- Have your after-care plan in action. Once you find your child--then what? Rehab? Jail? Counseling? How will school be handled? As you search for the reason why they left, be thinking about what you'll need to provide to correct the issue once you find them. Start making those calls and getting the approvals going. They take time.
- Eat, sleep, pray. Even if you don't feel like it, you must keep your strength and energy up.

WHAT TO HAVE OTHERS DO FOR YOU

- Run FB and social media
- Make poster, sharing on walls
- Checking local hangouts, driving the streets looking for the child. Make sure this person has a phone and can be reached by the person monitoring the social media pages. This way any leads can be followed up on real time. Having a few people on the streets on opposite ends of town allows for better immediate coverage.

WHAT TO WATCH FOR

- False information. Follow all leads, but be aware some information will be false. Any lead is a good lead and worth following, but it doesn't make every lead true. Some leads will simply give you information that leads you to better leads.